teenVirtue

YOUR QUESTIONS ANSWERED ABOUT
GOD, GUYS, AND GETTING OLDER

◄CONFIDENTIAL►

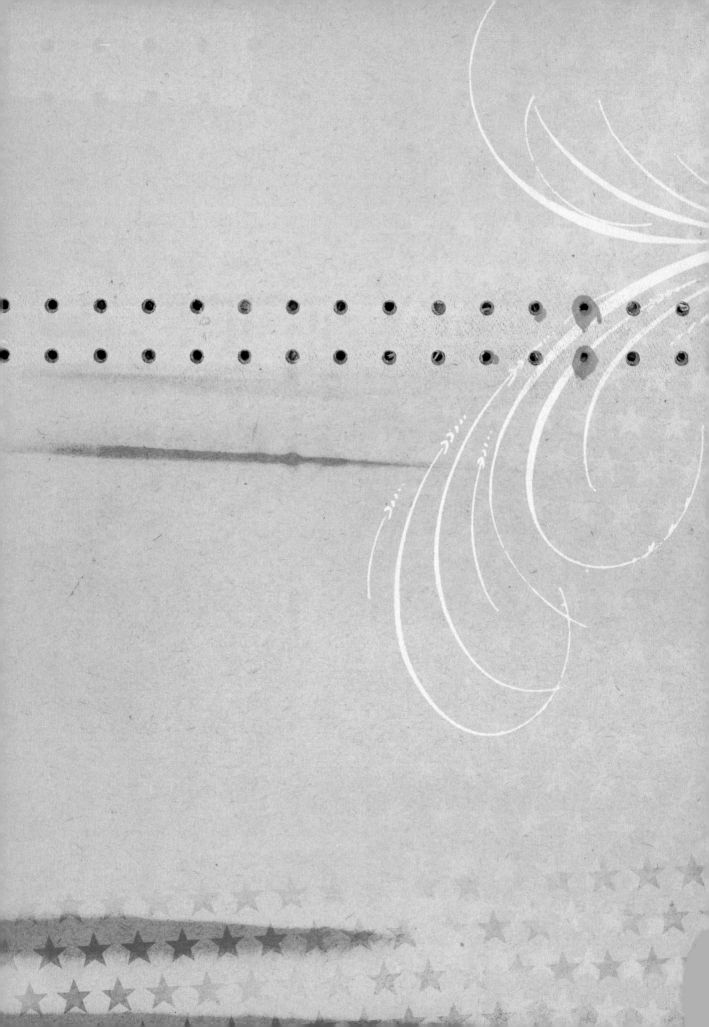

teenVirtue

CONFIDENTIAL

YOUR QUESTIONS ANSWERED ABOUT GOD, GUYS, AND GETTING OLDER

by vicki courtney

B&H
PUBLISHING GROUP

nashville, tennessee

TEENVIRTUE: REAL ISSUES, REAL LIFE.

**_TeenVirtue Confidential: Your Questions Answered about
God, Guys, and Getting Older_**

Copyright © 2007 by Vicki Courtney
All Rights Reserved.
Printed in the United States of America

Published by B&H Publishing Group, Nashville, Tennessee

ISBN: 978-0-8054-4192-5

Dewey Decimal Classification: 305.23
Subject Heading: TEENAGE GIRLS \ DATING (SOCIAL CUSTOMS) \
GIRLS—HEALTH AND HYGIENE

1 2 3 4 5 6 7 8 9 10   10 09 08 07

www.virtuousreality.com
NEW WEB SITE!

virtuousreallity.com is an online magazine for middle and high school girls. It receives visitors from all fifty states and over thirty countries! The site addresses topics teen girls face through relevant articles, an interactive blog, a question of the week feature, a prayer board, and much more.

Finally, there's a gathering place for girls just like you! While you're there, be sure to sign up for weekly updates. Also, if you're on MySpace, add us to your friend list: myspace.com/virtuous reality.com.

OTHER BOOKS BY VICKI COURTNEY
FROM B&H PUBLISHING GROUP

TeenVirtue: Real Issues, Real Life . . . A Teen Girl's Survival Guide

Your Boy: Raising a Godly Son in an Ungodly World

Your Girl: Raising a Godly Daughter in an Ungodly World

Yada Yada: A Devotional Journal for Moms

More Than Just Talk: A Journal for Girls

The Virtuous Woman: Shattering the Superwoman Myth

Between: A Girl's Guide to Life

TeenVirtue 2: A Teen Girl's Guide to Relationships

TABLE OF CONTENTS

1 Q's ABOUT THE FUTURE

2 Q's ABOUT GUYS

Q's ABOUT BODY DEVELOPMENT & SEX

3

Q's ABOUT FAITH

4

JUST CURIOUS

5

ABOUT THE AUTHORS

★ VICKI COURTNEY

Vicki Courtney is the founder of Virtuous Reality Ministries® that reaches more than one hundred fifty thousand girls and mothers a year. A mother herself of three teens, she seeks to provide both teens and their parents with the tools necessary to navigate today's promiscuous culture. She has done hundreds of radio and newspaper interviews and appeared on CNN, FOX News, and CNN Headline News to discuss issues impacting teens. She is the creator of VirtuousReality.com, an online magazine for teen girls, which has attracted visitors from all fifty states and over thirty countries. She is the author of the best-selling magabook, *TeenVirtue: Real Issues, Real Life . . . A Teen Girl's Survival Guide*, which won the 2006 ECPA Christian Book Award. Vicki resides in Austin, Texas, with her husband and three children. To learn more about Vicki Courtney, visit vickicourtney.com or myspace.com/vickicourtney.

★ SUSIE DAVIS

Susie Davis is a national speaker and author. She is the founder of Susie Davis Ministries, a resource, event and web-based ministry. Her books include *The Time of Your Life: Finding God's Rest in Your Busy Schedule* and *Loving Your Man without Losing Your Mind*. In addition, she collaborated on recent issues of *TeenVirtue* and *Between*. She and her husband Will, have three children: Will III, Emily, and Sara. For more information about Susie and her ministry visit www.susiedavisminstries.com.

★ A SPECIAL THANKS ALSO GOES TO:

Susan Jones, Sarah Kate Cameron, and Kristin Cameron who helped process the survey results and contributed their insight to several articles. A big thank you also goes to the girls who answered our survey questions and our fabulous guy panel!

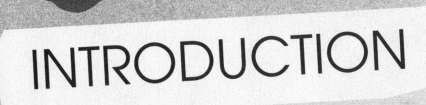

INTRODUCTION

No one ever said being a Christian is easy. Especially for a teen girl living in today's world. That's why this issue of *TeenVirtue* is all about *your* questions and *your* answers. I wanted to go straight to the heart of the average teen girl and address the topics that are on *your* mind. I surveyed nearly five hundred girls your age and asked them questions about friends, guys, God, and life in general. And boy, did they give answers! I also gave them an opportunity to ask questions that have been burning on their hearts. I think you'll be surprised to find that they ask many of the same questions you've had on your heart and mind.

But that's not all. If you're feeling left out since you didn't get to participate in the survey, you can still let your voice be heard! Log on to virtuousreality.com and you will find many of the same topics covered in *TeenVirtue Confidential*, as well as past issues of *TeenVirtue*. Some features even allow you to comment and give *your* two cents. What's *your* pet peeve? What's *your* most embarrassing moment? What's *your* question? Basically, the site was created to be a safe place for girls your age to come together—girls, by the way, who share *your* same values and beliefs.

TeenVirtue Confidential is more than just a trendy magazine-looking book. It's the beginning of a new revolution for godly virtue. And unless you've been hiding under a rock the past several years, you've probably noticed that we could use a little more virtue in this world. It seems like there's a new "girls gone wild" story in the news every day. Whether it's panti-less pop stars or beauty queens in rehab, girls from Hollywood to Hobocken (Yep, it's a real city!) are searching for meaning and purpose.

I've never claimed to have all the answers, but I do know the One who does. My heart's desire is that *TeenVirtue Confidential* will take you one step closer to the heart of God. And should that happen, forget the confidential part. It's a secret worth sharing!

—*Vicki Courtney*

Q's
ABOUT THE FUTURE

A Word About the Future

Jeremiah 6:16a

This is what the LORD says: "Stand at the crossroads and look; ask for the ancient paths, ask where the good way is, and walk in it, and you will find rest for your souls" (NIV).

Jeremiah 29:11

"For I know the plans I have for you," declares the LORD, "plans to prosper you and not to harm you, plans to give you hope and a future" (NIV).

Psalm 25:4–5

Show me your ways, O LORD, teach me your paths; guide me in your truth and teach me, for you are God my Savior, and my hope is in you all day long (NIV).

Proverbs 3:5–6

Trust in the LORD with all your heart and lean not on your own understanding; in all your ways acknowledge him, and he will make your paths straight (NIV).

Matthew 6:33

But seek ye first the kingdom of God, and his righteousness; and all these things shall be added unto you (KJV).

Ecclesiastes 8:7

Since no man knows the future, who can tell him what is to come?

Ecclesiastes 7:14

When times are good, be happy; but when times are bad, consider: God has made the one as well as the other. Therefore, a man cannot discover anything about his future (NIV).

Matthew 6:25-27

"Therefore I tell you, do not worry about your life, what you will eat or drink; or about your body, what you will wear. Is not life more important than food, and the body more important than clothes? Look at the birds of the air; they do not sow or reap or store away in barns, and yet your heavenly Father feeds them. Are you not much more valuable than they? Who of you by worrying can add a single hour to his life?" (NIV).

Matthew 28:19-20

Therefore go and make disciples of all nations, baptizing them in the name of the Father and of the Son and of the Holy Spirit, and teaching them to obey everything I have commanded you. And surely I am with you always, to the very end of the age (NIV).

Proverbs 24:14

Know also that wisdom is sweet to your soul; if you find it, there is a future hope for you, and your hope will not be cut off. (NIV) *

QUIZ:

who's running the show?

by Vicki Courtney

1. Drill Team tryouts are coming up and most of your friends are trying out. Dance and volleyball are your sports, but you can't do both so you have to choose between the two. You don't want to make a decision you will regret. You . . .

a) take out a sheet of paper and make two columns. You list the pros and cons of volleyball and drill team. Drill team wins—I mean, let's face it, the uniform is so much cuter.

b) ask your three closest friends what you should pick and go with the majority. Who cares what you really want to do, right?

c) take it before God and ask him to make it very clear to you. The Drill Team at your school is known for

their raunchy dance moves and God reminds you of this in your prayer time. Volleyball, here you come.

2. Rumor has it that a very cute boy in your youth group likes you. The problem is, he is known for being a player and a partier. You . . .

a) find out his screen name and look for him online. When he signs on, you make the first move. Half the girls in your youth group like this guy, so there's no time to waste!

b) analyze the possibility of the two of you being a couple with your best friend. She knows you better than anyone else, right?

c) pray for this guy. It's OK to develop a friendship, but the last thing he needs right now is a girlfriend. Besides, it doesn't sound like you're both on the same page spiritually, so dating is out.

3. You are summer job-hunting and filling out applications all over town. Most of the good jobs have been taken, but then you get a call from a great place wanting you to start next Sunday. You . . .

a) text at least ten of your friends letting them know that you got an awesome job.

b) call your best friend to see if she also got the job, since you applied at the same time. The two of you do everything together.

c) graciously decline. You had no idea that working on Sunday was part of the deal. Besides, God will honor your commitment to set aside his day for worship.

4. You eat, sleep, and breathe cheerleading. You were a cheerleader last year and pretty much a shoe in for Varsity

next year. Tryouts come and amazingly, you don't make it. You find out that you were a half point shy of making the squad. You . . .

a) cry yourself to sleep that night. You can't imagine life without a megaphone and pom-poms. The next day, you sign up for cheer classes so you'll be ready for next year.

b) ask your mom to call the sponsor and get the scores. Who knows, maybe she can work her magic and get you on the squad.

c) are disappointed and shed a few tears. In the end, you go to God and acknowledge your disappointment. You prayed about the whole thing and you came to the conclusion that God knows what he's doing even if it doesn't make much sense now.

5. It's time to decide on the college you will attend. You . . .

a) will probably go with the one that just "feels right."

b) will head in the direction most of your friends are going.

c) will pray about it and go with the one that brings you the most peace in your heart. God knows best, right?

SELF-PACED PROGRAM (MOSTLY A): You are in charge of your destiny. Your "take charge" attitude can be an admirable quality as long as you are relying on God first to lead you. When you take him out of the picture and run the show, it's only a matter of time before you will find yourself outside of his will and purpose for your life.

FRIENDS AND FAMILY PLAN (MOSTLY B): You rely on others to steer you in the right direction rather than God. Your friends and family can't possibly know you like God does. Sometimes, God uses others to help steer us in the right direction, but if you haven't given the matter over to him, it will be hard to tell whether or not you are getting man's mere opinion or God-inspired wisdom.

FATHER KNOWS BEST (MOSTLY C): When it comes to your future, it looks like you are accustomed to God running the show. You are to be commended for leaning on God at such a young age. When it comes to extremely important matters such as your career path, who you will marry, and other life choices, you will be less likely to stray from his plan and purpose for your life.

Jeremiah 6:16 says, "Stand at the crossroads and look; ask for the ancient paths, ask where the good way is and walk in it and you will find rest for your souls." The next time you find yourself at a crossroads in life, remember that promise! ✱

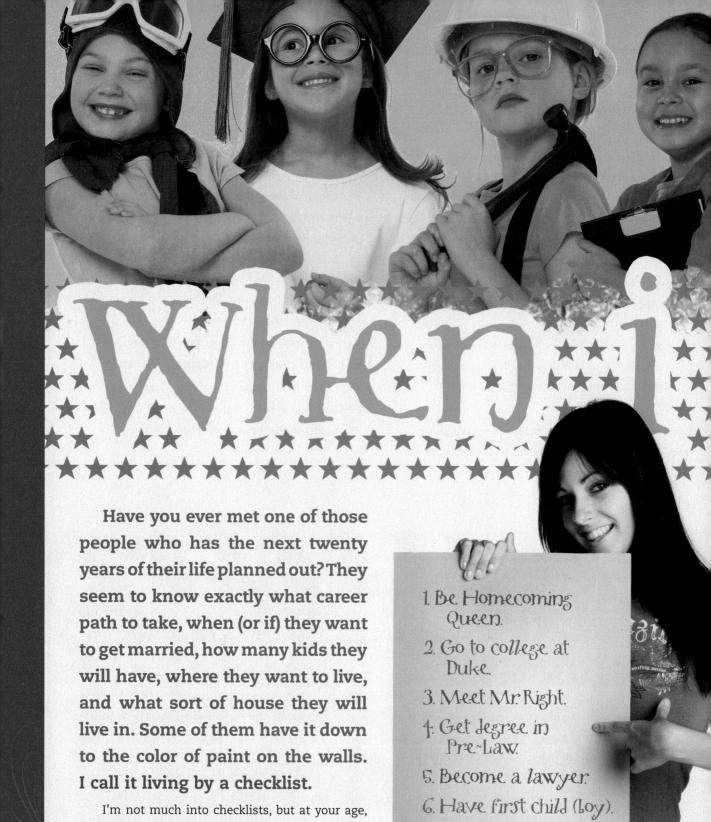

When i

Have you ever met one of those people who has the next twenty years of their life planned out? They seem to know exactly what career path to take, when (or if) they want to get married, how many kids they will have, where they want to live, and what sort of house they will live in. Some of them have it down to the color of paint on the walls. I call it living by a checklist.

I'm not much into checklists, but at your age, I was fairly certain that I had it all figured out, at least when it came to a career. I wanted to be a lawyer. In fact, when I got to college, I declared myself a "Pre-Law major." That lasted all of about one semester and then I changed my major to Business, then Communications, then Sociology, and then Economics. OK, so maybe I didn't have it all figured out after all.

1. Be Homecoming Queen.
2. Go to college at Duke.
3. Meet Mr. Right.
4. Get degree in Pre-Law.
5. Become a lawyer.
6. Have first child (boy).
7. Make Partner.
8. Have second child (girl).
9. Retire at 55.
10. Live Happily Ever After.

Grow up

★★★ by vicki courtney ★★★

After five years in college and changing my major five times, I finally graduated with a degree in Economics. A career counselor told me that most people with degrees in Economics pursue jobs in the banking industry. Hmmm. I had spent a lot of time in banks in my college years, but it was usually to sort out my bounced checks. Probably not a good field for me, considering I couldn't even balance my own checkbook. Fast forward twenty years later and I still can't balance a checkbook. Thank goodness I didn't go to work in a bank because I might not have figured out that I was supposed to be a writer all along.

And do you know how I figured out that I was supposed to be a writer? After I was married and had my first child, I began sending out one of those annual Christmas letters every year to my friends and family. I always hated getting Christmas letters from people who had perfect kids and perfect lives. You know, the ones where "Little Johnny just turned one and can sing his ABCs in English, Spanish, and French, blind-folded while tap dancing." The next year the letter informs us he's getting recruitment letters from the ivy leagues colleges. They may as well just skip all the bragging and get to the real reason they are sending the letter—they just want to say, "Nanny, nanny, boo-boo— we're better than you!"

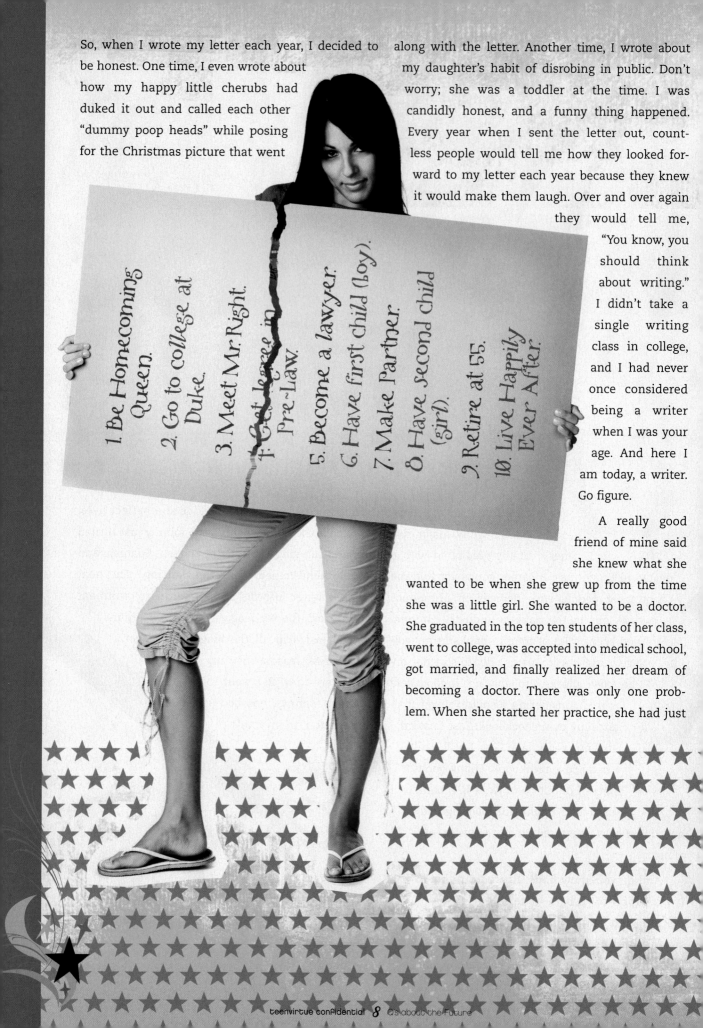

So, when I wrote my letter each year, I decided to be honest. One time, I even wrote about how my happy little cherubs had duked it out and called each other "dummy poop heads" while posing for the Christmas picture that went along with the letter. Another time, I wrote about my daughter's habit of disrobing in public. Don't worry; she was a toddler at the time. I was candidly honest, and a funny thing happened. Every year when I sent the letter out, countless people would tell me how they looked forward to my letter each year because they knew it would make them laugh. Over and over again they would tell me, "You know, you should think about writing." I didn't take a single writing class in college, and I had never once considered being a writer when I was your age. And here I am today, a writer. Go figure.

A really good friend of mine said she knew what she wanted to be when she grew up from the time she was a little girl. She wanted to be a doctor. She graduated in the top ten students of her class, went to college, was accepted into medical school, got married, and finally realized her dream of becoming a doctor. There was only one problem. When she started her practice, she had just

1. Be Homecoming Queen.
2. Go to college at Duke.
3. Meet Mr. Right.
4. Get degree in Pre-Law.
5. Become a lawyer.
6. Have first child (boy).
7. Make Partner.
8. Have second child (girl).
9. Retire at 55.
10. Live Happily Ever After.

had her first child. As the days went on, it became harder and harder for her to leave her baby with the nanny so she could have her "dream job." She stuck with her "checklist," but was torn. That is, until one day when she came home and the nanny told her not to fix any more bottles for the baby. The nanny informed her that she had weaned the baby from the bottle and taught him to drink from a cup. That was really tough on my friend because she wanted to be the one to experience her baby's first milestones. The straw that broke the camel's back came a couple months later when the nanny informed her he had taken his first steps and my friend had missed it. She told me that it was at that point she realized no matter how careful she had been to plan the details of her future, she had not factored in how she might feel as a mother when pursuing her lifelong dream job. Today, she still practices medicine, but only part-time. She has other important matters to tend to like soccer games and trips to the park. She also had two more kids and made sure she was around to see their first milestones.

My point is this: it's impossible to plan for the future and factor in all the details when you don't have all the details. Resist the urge to draw a road map for your life. If you live your life by a checklist, it allows God little room to direct your steps. There is nothing wrong with having an idea of what you might like your future to be, but don't go overboard in micromanaging every detail. Besides, God may not see eye-to-eye with everything on your checklist. Or, as my friend learned, he may add something to the list that is dreamier than that dream job. Leave room for God to move in your life. There is plenty of time for him to reveal his plan and purpose for your life. In the meantime, sit tight and enjoy the ride.★

We can make our plans, but the LORD determines our steps. (Proverbs 16:9 NLT)

Act Your

One thing that saddens me for teen girls today is the constant pressure you face to grow up way too fast.

I was struck by this fact one day when flipping through a vintage copy of *Seventeen* magazine from the early 1980s, which just so happens to be when I was a teenager. I laughed when I saw an ad for sleepwear. There was a cheesy picture of teen girls at a sleepover with a bowl of popcorn and a big behemoth-sized record player in the center of the room and they were dancing in their flannel floor-length nightgowns trimmed in white lace. I remember begging my mom for a Lanz nightgown just like the ones in the ad. Fast forward to today and girls your age wearing pjs more suitable for your honeymoon and married years. Last year my sixteen-year-old daughter's cheerleading squad had a Christmas party where they drew names and exchanged gifts. I couldn't believe how many girls received intimate underwear from Victoria's Secret. When I got engaged, I could hardly wait to go to Victoria's Secret and register for lingerie for my upcoming lingerie shower. It was just understood that you didn't set foot into the store until you had an engagement ring on. Now, when you step into a Victoria's Secret store, you are greeted with display after display of colorful thong

AGE!!!

(C'MON, YOU KNOW YOU WANT TO)

BY VICKI COURTNEY

underwear and sexy boy cut shorts geared to girls your age. In fact, you don't even have to go to a lingerie store to get sexy lingerie. It's in all the trendy teen retail stores, many times in the coed stores, right by the checkout where it's no big deal for guys to see the display.

In addition to the pressure to wear grown-up lingerie is the added pressure to wear immodest clothes that encourage girls to cultivate sensualities that, again, were meant to be saved for the wedding night. And then there's the hip-hop music with its clear message that your body is meant to be nothing more than a tool for the gratification of men. That's probably why your mom and dad "overreact" when they hear you humming along to some of the songs on the radio. Then there are TV shows with adult themes like The OC and Desperate Housewives which are popular among teen

> ## IS IT ANY WONDER THAT MANY GIRLS YOUR AGE SAID IN A SURVEY THAT THEY "MISS BEING LITTLE"
> ## ?

girls. Is it any wonder that many girls your age said in a survey that they "miss being little"? It's like you jumped straight from little girl to adult woman. One day you had the Barbies out and the next day you're begging your mom for thong underwear.

You might wonder if it's even possible to "act your age" in a culture that demands you to grow up fast. Well, there's good news—it is possible. In fact, my sixteen-year-old daughter is often teased by her friends for having an obsession with the Disney Channel. Her "sweet sixteen" birthday cake even had the Disney Channel logo on it. I'm telling you, the girl drops everything for a Hannah Montana and Suite Life double marathon. She does not dress immodest and understands that many guys read more into a revealing outfit than just a simple fashion statement. You may be thinking, *bless her heart—she must be a nerdy wall flower with no friends and nothing better to do!* Not hardly. She has more friends than I can

ARE YOU IN A HURRY TO GROW UP? HANG ON TO YOUR GIRLHOOD!

count. She is a Varsity Cheerleader at her school and well-liked. She is beautiful both inside and out. I have even thought about praying that she will revert back to her toddler days where she had a bit of a nose-picking problem. Anything to help ward off the boys! Maybe the Disney Channel obsession will keep them at bay. Now, does this mean she is perfect and never listens to pop music or shops at Victoria's Secret? Nope. I can't seem to get her to pick up the flannel nightgown habit. But, she has at least retained some of her "girlhood" by resisting the temptation to dress immodestly and watch shows where everyone's hooking up on a regular basis.

So, what about you? Are you in a hurry to grow up? Hang on to your girlhood. Trust me, one day you will look back and wish you had enjoyed every possible moment of this fleeting no-longer-a-child-but-not-yet-a-woman season of life. Don't be ashamed to be young. Watch Saturday morning cartoons. Pull out your old Barbies just for fun when a friend comes over. She's probably way overdue for an outfit change anyway. Have a water gun fight with your friends or some of the younger kids in your neighborhood. Look at an old photo album of your baby and toddler years. Put your old Little Mermaid sheets on your bed. Wear braids. Dig that worn and ratty looking stuffed bear from your baby years out of your closet and put it on a shelf in your room or better yet, your bed. Get that shoebox down with your old notes from friends from the pre-IM days and read them. Get out your old stickers and make a card for your mom. Braid friendship bracelets for your friends. Next time it clouds up, call a friend to come over and play in the rain. For extra credit, build a mud castle. Resist the temptation to grow up so fast. As my daughter, Paige would say, "Who needs The OC when you can watch a quality show like High School Musical?"

You who are young, make the most of your youth. Relish your youthful vigor. Follow the impulses of your heart. If something looks good to you, pursue it. But know also that not just anything goes; You have to answer to God for every last bit of it. (Ecclesiastes 11:9 The Message) ✱

SURVEY: WORDS OF WISDOM FROM COLLEGE WOMEN

Below you will find words of wisdom from college women who have been in your shoes and know a thing or two about the pressures you face on a daily basis. Proverbs 3:13–14 says, "Blessed is the man who finds wisdom, the man who gains understanding, for she is more profitable than silver and yields better returns than gold" (NIV). As they share their hearts, take heed to their advice, learn from their mistakes, and apply their words of wisdom to your remaining middle school and high school years. Who knows, you may be the one handing out wisdom someday!

Meet the College Panel

Shelley: Auburn University
Secondary Education, 2006

Traci: Baylor University
Marketing/Public Relations, 2009

Stephanie: Columbus State University
Nursing, 2008

Anna: Baylor University
Undecided, 2009

Courtney: Auburn University
Rehabilitation Services Education, 2007

Beth: University of Mobile
Sociology, 2008

Kristen: University of Texas
English, Human Development and
Family Sciences, 2008

Ellen: Ringling School of Art and Design
Illustration, 2008

Kristin: Auburn University
Accounting, 2008

Shelley: If I could go back to high school, I would befriend the students who didn't have friends. I think there is so much pressure in high school to be in the "popular" crowd, that a lot of really amazing people get overlooked by people who could befriend them. I know I wish I had befriended more people who were different than me in high school. My perspective of life was so narrow at that time.

Courtney: If I could change one decision about high school, it would have been to take on more challenges to better prepare myself for challenges ahead.

Anna: I would change my idea that not doing "bad things" was enough to be considered a good Christian witness. I would speak and act what I was thinking on the inside.

Beth: I would not have been so busy. I would have spent more time with closer friends and family instead of killing myself to do too many things.

Stephanie: I would change the way I responded to peer pressure. I would not give in so easily or try to make myself fit in with the "in" crowd.

Kristen: My biggest regret is that I didn't stick to a break up with my boyfriend during my senior year. Instead I allowed myself to be dragged back into a situation where I lost my spiritual focus. It was a cyclical loss of respect, and I wish I had been strong enough to re-identify my self-worth in God alone.

Ellen: Generally, I think I was way too worried about how other people viewed me and not as worried about how God viewed me.

Traci: I honestly wouldn't change anything. I believe I am where I am today because of the decisions I made. I think God puts us at our lowest low to get to our highest high. But if I could change one thing, I would have cherished my relationships with my friends and family more. In high school, I was always going and I never took the time to really soak up my family and friends. Now that I am in college, I am really seeing how important it is to embrace your family and friends.

Anna: Seek God's face. Seek his joy. Don't be fooled by Satan's attempts to show you happiness in boys, popularity, or the perfect image, because although the pursuit of those things may be fun and seem harmless, it is a tough habit to break. And outside the world of high school, the stakes increase, and the costs are more painful.

Ellen: Make time for your family, friends, and for spending time with God.

Kristen: Think for yourself. Be original—it's more fun! Don't blindly follow what your friends say or do.

Beth: Choose your battles wisely. Realize there's a much bigger world out there than your own.

Shelley: Love on everyone. Once you graduate and you realize that there's more out there than just YOU, especially as a Christian, you realize that all the petty "popularity contests" and snobbery is not what pleases God. Once high school is over, you realize that no one really cares if you were "best dressed," "most popular," or "best looking." At that point, you realize it's all about how you treated others, and if you showed the love of Christ to them.

Traci: Build a core relationship with the Lord because in college, the waters are rough. You need a firm foundation now. College is the biggest test of faith I have encountered.

Stephanie: Be yourself. Don't try to be like everyone else because you will constantly have to be changing to fit into their mold. Be proud of who you are and who you will become.

Kristin: Don't stress out about the little stuff. Middle school and high school will be over before you know it, so work hard and have fun.

Are you still really good friends with your high school friends or have your relationships changed as you've moved on to college?

Anna: They have all changed. Some are better, some are worse, and some are just different.

Ellen: In my experience, the friendships that I really valued in high school have stood the test of time. Most of the people I hang out with on a day-to-day basis have changed simply because I moved to a different place.

Traci: My relationships have changed. In college you are able to make friends with whoever you want because you have a larger variety of people to be friends with. So you can really find who you fit with. You develop a deeper bond with your college friends . . . you are with these people twenty-four hours a day, seven days a week so you see them in every aspect.

Shelley: I am still friends with most of my best high school friends. However, I have made many wonderful friends at college who mean the world to me. They are strong in their faith. We talk, encourage, and pray with and for one another. I think the friends I've made after high school are truer friends because in college you get to choose your friends. There's not a certain "crowd" that you are trying to "fit in," especially at a big college.

Beth: Most of my relationships have changed. I'm friends with most of my high school friends, but I have made many more deep and meaningful relationships with people in college. However, my best friend today is still my best friend from high school.

Courtney: Since I changed high schools a couple of times, I only have one or two really good friends from those days. All of the other closer relationships I've made have been at college.

Kristen: I happen to go to school with two of my best friends and it's such a blessing. I've made new friends in college (some probably not a great influence) but those two best friends keep me completely grounded. They help to wake me up from getting sucked in to it all because we can afford to be brutally honest with each other when needed. Keeping up a network with people who have known you for years can be so helpful.

What do you miss the most about being in middle or high school?

Stephanie: I miss being able to be with my friends and bonding with all my classmates. You may not think it is important in middle or high school, but you will realize it is when you graduate and aren't able to see all your friends as much as you used to.

Courtney: I miss the outlook I had when I was younger, the way I trusted and took everything as it was.

Beth: I miss the easy classes! Everything takes much more time in college. I also miss soccer a lot.

Shelley: I miss just hanging out, not having any worries. Parents paying for everything, cooking the meals, doing the laundry, and I got to play. There was no serious responsibility and responsibility is scary! So I miss the simplicity of life.

Anna: I miss how comfortable and familiar everything felt.

Traci: I miss how easy it was! I didn't realize how hard college would be. Not just studies but being on your own and having no parents waking you up or making you lunch, etc. It's a lot harder than I expected but still amazing and I have grown up so much!

Kristin: I miss the simplicity of life. Sure, there was always drama, but it was over petty issues like boys and clothes. Being in college,

I am fully responsible for myself and all of the decisions I make. My parents aren't around to give me sound advice on everything and I have to make the tough decisions on my own. I can call home to talk things through with them, but ultimately everything is up to me. But, as much as I might miss the simplicity sometimes, I would never trade where I am now to go back to middle school or high school. God has taught me so much over these past two years and I have grown in so many ways.

Ellen: I really love college, so it's hard to think of what I miss. I guess I miss not having so many responsibilities.

How has being away from home and away from your parents changed your relationship with God?

Shelley: Since I've been away from home, my relationship with God has definitely been strengthened. There's nothing like being away from home for the first time and realizing that you now have a huge responsibility on your shoulders. The comfort level is gone. It's really scary. But, at the same time, God has used it for good in my life because it caused me to seek hard after him and to trust him with all things. When I realize that I have nothing else, it is then that I truly realize he is all I need.

Stephanie: Being away from home has strengthened my relationship with God.

Kristen: The dynamic of college has changed my relationship with God. There's an intense temptation all the time. But it completely goes back to your support system and faith. Surrounding yourself with people who get drunk frequently is asking for trouble. That's looking for temptation. I had to seek out Christian girls who shared my same values and beliefs. And knowing that there was a group of people praying for me everyday, girls that were keeping me accountable, is a definite comfort. It helped to stabilize my faith because I felt God's love through them.

Beth: It has strengthened my relationship with him so much more than I could ever have imagined. I have learned to be more dependent upon him than anyone else. I have learned more about him and more about myself because loneliness, intimidation, and insecurity are always around. Therefore, crying out to him has made my relationship with him much more personal.

Anna: It has forced me to take ownership of my personal walk with Christ.

Kristin: When I moved to college, I didn't know anybody at school and it was so intimidating. I had to completely rely on God to get through the first few weeks. In the past two years, I have really been able to give God control of everything and have allowed him to grow and stretch me. My faith and my relationship with God is definitely much stronger now than it was in high school.

Courtney: Being away from home and my parents has greatly increased my relationship with Daddy (my heavenly Father). Never before had I leaned on him as I have in the past three years here. And I wouldn't trade that for anything in the world!

Ellen: It really has given me the freedom to honestly question and discover what is good and true about my relationship with God. It also has driven me to depend on him more.

Traci: It has really taught me to be dependent on God. Before, when something went wrong, I had my parents there to hold me and comfort me. But now, I have learned how to crawl up into the arms of my maker and let him dry my tears. And let me tell you, he does the best job! ★

How I Knew My Husband Was *The One*

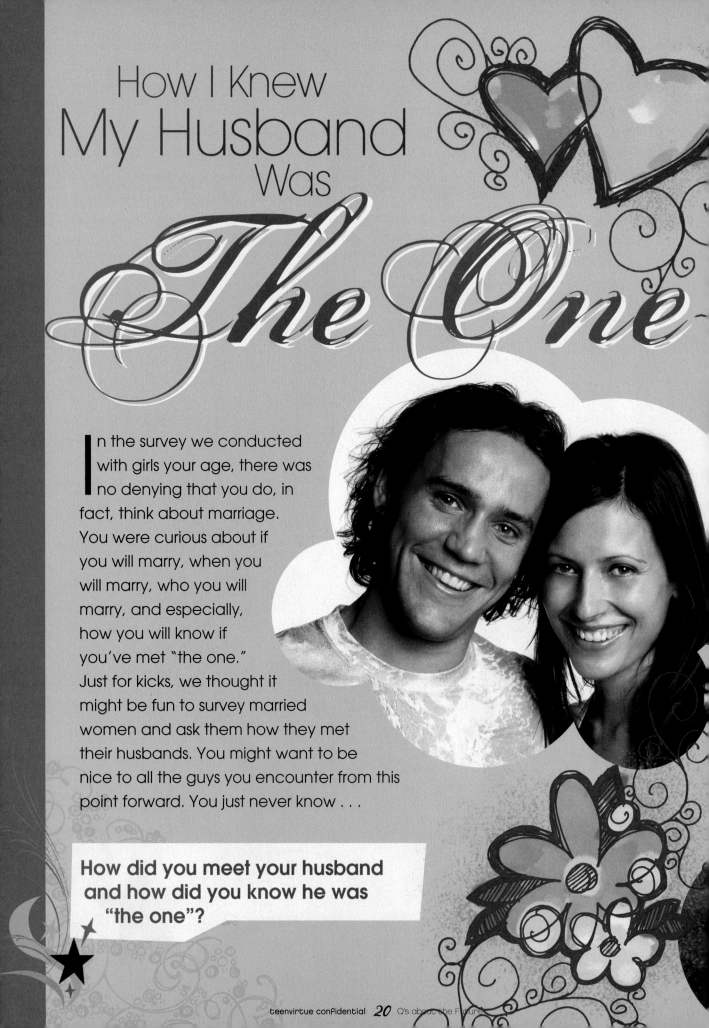

In the survey we conducted with girls your age, there was no denying that you do, in fact, think about marriage. You were curious about if you will marry, when you will marry, who you will marry, and especially, how you will know if you've met "the one." Just for kicks, we thought it might be fun to survey married women and ask them how they met their husbands. You might want to be nice to all the guys you encounter from this point forward. You just never know . . .

How did you meet your husband and how did you know he was "the one"?

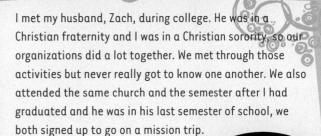

I met my husband in 7th grade choir at my church. We became great friends and remained the closest of friends throughout junior high and high school. We never dated. I'm sure he had reasons why, but mine are: I had a rule that I absolutely would not date anyone who weighed less than me! I lovingly refer to Jimmy in high school as the coolest Eagle Scout in the band. Sixteen years later, we met to plan our class reunion. He had grown seven inches and was a "man." Still, we didn't date until we were almost thirty, when he finally suggested we go on a date! It had never occurred to me to date him. But on that "date" he told me he was in love with me, and although I was totally freaked out, it didn't take me long to figure out that he truly was the one for me.

— Rhonda, married 11 years

I met my husband when I was a junior in high school and he was a sophomore. We had study hall together. I had "heard" that he had a crush on me, but we remained good friends through high school and went our separate ways for college. We managed to see each other when home for breaks. I knew that he was more than a friend to me when a college friend of mine expressed interest in him. I was hit with a surge of jealousy. We began dating shortly after that and married 2 1/2 years later. He has been my best friend for as long as I can remember!

— Alison, married 17 years

I met my husband, Zach, during college. He was in a Christian fraternity and I was in a Christian sorority, so our organizations did a lot together. We met through those activities but never really got to know one another. We also attended the same church and the semester after I had graduated and he was in his last semester of school, we both signed up to go on a mission trip. I had just ended a bad relationship and was looking forward to spending time with God and getting away from "boys" on this trip. Zach had just ended a serious relationship and didn't want to date any-one. On this trip God did so many things and showed me a lot about myself. I got up in front of the group (100 people) one night to share my experiences. I was so excited and was sharing all God had done that day and everyone was staring at me with blank faces, except for Zach. He looked at me and smiled with joy in his face. He understood what I was saying and was happy for me. Throughout the rest of the trip we talked about our experiences and enjoyed each other's company. I remember coming back from the trip anxious to tell people what God had done and to tell them about hanging out with Zach. We have talked every day since that mission trip.

— Joy, married 5 years

I met my husband at a Halloween costume party. I was dressed in full clown costume and make-up. He had no idea what I looked like or what shape I was, but he asked for my phone number! I found that pretty special. I'm not sure when I "knew" he was the one but I was immediately drawn to his sense of humor and his compassionate heart.

— Leilani, married 16 years

I was hanging out in a park with a group of friends when this guy drove past us. I saw him, but he did not see me. I told myself at that moment, *That's the guy I am going to marry.* My friend knew who he was because she knew his friends. Without telling her my purpose, I convinced my friend to throw a big St. Patrick's Day party and told her to invite him and his friends. I watched for him all night and when I saw him, I pinched him because he was not wearing green. We were both seniors in high school, getting ready to graduate. We married five years later.

— Betty, married 23 years

I met my husband when we were on a university retreat. We were both part of the same college department at our church. A friend of mine on the retreat asked me to come with her to see this guy on the bus who "she was wanting to date." We got on the bus and there he was tying his shoes, and that's when I knew. He looked up to say hello and I melted. Unfortunately, he was the same person my friend wanted to date. So, of course, I didn't pursue him, but in the back of my mind I knew that someday we would be married. Several months later, after much prodding from my brother (unbeknownst to me), he asked me out. It was exactly eighteen months from our first date to our wedding date! God is good! — **Kathy, married 15 years**

I met my husband, Bill, when I was only six years old. He was five years old and my neighbor. As children, we made mud pies together, played "spy" and watched Road Runner and Wile E. Coyote. He moved away for several years and we began to write each other when we were teenagers. I had written a letter to God one night, telling him that I would not pursue boys. I wanted to wait for "the one." I had a desire to be in youth ministry, as well. Two weeks after I wrote that letter, Bill showed up at my doorstep! He was in town for a surprise visit. As we talked, he began to share his vision for youth ministry and I knew at that moment that he was the one! We got married at the tender ages of eighteen and nineteen. — **Tracie, married 15 years**

We lived down the street from each other. I had to pass by his house every day on my way to school. I don't know when I knew he was the one, but he says he knew the first time he saw me. — **Stace, married 12 years**

He was a family friend and his mother was the delivery room nurse when I was born. We knew about each other, but we really didn't know each other. When we were old enough to date, my aunt got us together. I knew on our first date that he was going to be "the one"! We went out to dinner, and I talked the entire time . . . and I'm not a talker. I guess nerves got the best of me. On the way home, he asked me if I would sit next to him in his truck. He didn't "expect" me to sit by him (or anything else) because he bought me dinner. That impressed me so much that I decided right then and there that I would marry him. We got engaged six months later and were married one year later. :) — **Cindy, married 17 years**

I met my husband when I went on a date with one of his friends. It was very clear that the friend and I were not a match, but he was kind enough to say "You should meet my friend Mark." He introduced us and we liked each other from the start. — **Lisa, married 10 years**

I met my husband on a blind date in college. I think I knew he was "the one" when I thought of him all the time. I talked to him on the phone and didn't want to hang up. We always had a hard time saying good-bye! — **Janice, married 17 years**

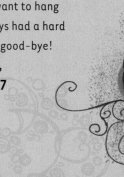

I met my husband when I moved in next door to him! He worked for the architect that built the duplexes he lived in and had jokingly told the gal who rented them out that only a cute single girl could move in next door. When I went to check out the duplex that was for rent, she brought me outside on the driveway to discuss the details. Jim was in the window and gave her the thumbs up sign. She then told me that the other duplexes had already been leased and that was the only one left so I took it! I didn't find out until about six years later that Jim had set that up!!! We went on our first date, got engaged three weeks later, got married four months later, and just celebrated our twentieth anniversary. — **Kristi, married 20 years**

I was set up with my husband by a four-year-old! I was teaching at a Christian school and coaching cheerleading. One evening, while coaching, a man stuck his head in the gym and asked where the Boy Scouts were meeting. I wasn't sure but helped him find them. He was good looking but I assumed he was someone's father. I didn't know it at the time but he was picking up his nephew. When he took his nephew home, he asked who the teacher was that helped him find the Boy Scouts and said that he wished he could go out with me. The next day the preschool teacher came to me and said that one of her students (the man's nephew) wanted to talk to me. The little boy told me, "My uncle is in love with you and wants your phone number." Laughingly I gave it to him, thinking it would never reach his uncle. He took it home and told his dad that night that he needed to call Uncle Brad. He gave him my number, he called, and we talked and laughed on the phone for an hour. I knew after our first date that he was "the one." — **Lisa, married 16 years**

We both lived in Jester Dorm at the University of Texas. My next-door neighbor at the dorm invited me to eat Sunday supper with her and "this cute guy." Well, the cute guy was also very nice and funny and he invited me to a Paul Simon concert the next week. I knew he was "the one" when he listened to my life story and still said it didn't matter. It was the first time in my life that I experienced unconditional love.
— **Vicki, married 29 years**

I met my husband at a church roller-skating function. He didn't usually come to church events but I'm glad he came to that one! He was Mr. Popular and I couldn't believe he was interested in me. I can't say I knew he was the one; I just knew that I wanted to be his wife.
— **Rhonda, married 27 years**

My husband and I always joke that God was giving us three opportunities to meet. We attended college 100 miles apart and have pictures of us sitting at ball games a few rows away from each other, but we did not meet in college. My best friend's husband and my "boyfriend" at the time just happened to work at the same place as my future husband, but we did not meet through friends. God sent him away from his hometown in Texas to Colorado to start his career. I had just moved back

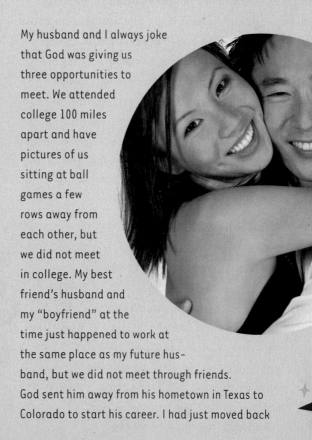

home to Colorado after graduating from college in Texas, and we ended up meeting each other at church! When meeting Scot for the first time, I had a silent conversation with God. I remember thinking, Lord, this is him, isn't it? We started dating shortly after and things progressed from there. **— Heather, married 13 years**

I met my husband at the radio station where he worked as a disc jockey. My best friend since the fourth grade, Noel, and I were coming back from shopping at the mall and I drove past the radio station to see if we could get a song played for us. John was outside just arriving for his shift. He and Noel had worked together so she introduced me. He ended up playing the song we wanted and after I took her home, I went back to the station to say thank you and he asked for my phone number. I told him my number, but he didn't have any paper so I didn't believe he would remember it. Well, he remembered my number and called me. I knew he was "the one" when after meeting him, every other guy I met couldn't measure up. None were as nice, caring, thoughtful, or good looking as John. We went steady two months later, got engaged two years later, and we have been married for twenty-nine years this past April. My husband, John, is truly a gift from the Lord and still tells me he loves me every day! **— Marilyn, married 29 years**

I met my husband working in a restaurant. He ordered, "Two Chevy Specials with cheese and an order of french fries." Funny I still remember what he ordered. I knew he was the one when he took me out to his parents pasture and walked me to the middle of a dried-up tank and asked me to marry him, NOW! He said he couldn't wait . . . We were married one week later. We are more in love with each other now than ever. I hope and pray that my daughter finds someone just like her dad. **— Georgia, married 18 years**

I met my husband when I was twenty. It was the summer before my senior year of college and I had an internship at his company. I had a crush on him over the summer and had told my roommates, but he never asked me out over the summer or acted unprofessional in any way. We ran into each other again in November, the week of my twenty-first birthday, and he called and asked me out. On our first date, we talked for hours in his car out in front of my sorority house when he dropped me off. He never once even tried to kiss me. I knew by our third date that he was "the one" because he drove up to my parents' house (an hour and a half away) over the Christmas holiday to meet my parents, sister, aunt, grandparents, and my ninety-five-year-old great grandma (and they all loved him!). We got engaged in one year and married six months later. **— Amy, married 13 years**

I met my husband while applying for a job with the company that he was working for at the time. I was looking at a large aerial photograph of our city when he came walking in with a bunch of other guys. They were all laughing and being really loud, and my future "husband" let out a really big burp! I thought, What a pig! We have a big laugh about that now! I didn't know until about a year later that he was "the one." He had a lot of "making up" to do after that burp. **— Dawn, married 11 years**

I met my husband, Marty, at Fort Campbell, Kentucky. We were both in the military, working on an airfield. I knew he was "the one" when he took me to his family reunion and I met his entire family. We really enjoyed that vacation, and he asked me to marry him before we headed back to Fort Campbell. We married soon after, and within a month both of us had deployed to Saudi Arabia for an unplanned nine-month "honeymoon" apart! With God's protection, we made it home safely and have been happily married ever since. — **Ava, married 15 years**

I met my husband at a gas/car-wash station. I was getting out to wash off the back of my mom's car and he ran over to help me. While my mom went through the car wash in the car, I stayed and talked to Rick, my now husband. I was fifteen at the time and he was seventeen. Two weeks later we came through the same station again and this time he asked my mom for my phone number. I was very surprised to watch her give it to him as she did not know him at all. He called me several times before I even got home and since I was only fifteen and not allowed to date until I was sixteen, we got to know each other through my youth group events. He was not a Christian when we met but became one through my family and our youth pastor's teachings. I knew he was "the one" almost a month after we met. Don't really know how . . .I just knew. We got married three years later. It has not been easy marrying at such a young age. We give God all the credit for keeping us together. Today, we work as youth pastors together in full-time ministry. — **Judy, married 29 years**

I met my husband while I was working at a restaurant and he was a customer. When I looked into his eyes, I pictured us sitting on a swing when we were seventy and I knew he was the one. — **Saymme, married 6 years**

I met my husband when I was a telephone operator and he placed a collect phone call. The person he was calling never answered the phone and so we just kept on talking. A couple of weeks later I was transferred to a different division of the phone company and I was told to report to my new boss's office, who just so happened to be the father of the man I had talked to on the phone. That night I began dating his son. I knew he was "the one" because of all the coincidences that brought us together—I felt God was pointing us toward one another. — **Julie, married 25 years**

I met my husband while we were both working in a grocery store. I was checking groceries and he was bagging them. He was very polite and helpful to all the customers (and to me!). I noticed that he always put other people's needs ahead of his own and that's how I knew he was "the one"! — **Kym, married 18 years**

I met my husband on the set of the TV show, "Dallas," which was very popular in the 70s and 80s. He was an actor and I was a model. We were both "extras" that day. I knew he was "the one" on our first date when he was such a gentleman opening doors and being so chivalrous. We married three years later! — **Kelli, married 17 years**

I met my husband on a plane on the way to the Bahamas. We sat in the same row across from each other. Everybody was pretty much watching the movie on the plane and all the shades on the windows were down so it was pretty dark. My "future" husband was the only one with his light on doing work. The movie had a very happy ending, but it was a tearjerker. So with my head phones on I could not hear myself, and I cried at the end. I felt as if someone was staring at me so I looked over and he was watching me. I got up to go get a tissue and he said, "Good movie, huh?!" and I replied, "Yes, great movie." Then I introduced myself and we got to know each other on the cruise. I returned home. I lived in Wisconsin at the time and he lived in California. When I arrived home and went to work the next day, there were a dozen red roses waiting for me, and the message read, "I hope your day is as bright as you make mine. Love, Rick!" It's history from there—eleven days after we met he told me he loved me, a month later I moved to California, and a month after that we were married. — **Anissa, married 11 years** ✶

YOUR QUESTIONS ABOUT THE FUTURE

by SUSIE DAVIS

Will I Be Happy?

Gosh I hope so. I would love for you always to feel happy. But the truth is the things that make us happy change all the time, and the things that we think will make us happy aren't always the things that are best for us. For example, when I was in high school I felt sure that I could be happy if I could just weigh a certain amount (which on looking back, was not a healthy weight) or get a certain guy (looking back, not the best choice). I thought I would be happy if I could get some recognition for being popular by getting elected "friendliest" or "most beautiful." And while some of those things did roll my way when I was in high school, the happy meter in my life didn't always stay full. For instance, when I got elected cheerleader (which I begged God for and told him it would make me oh so happy) that didn't mean that I stayed happy. Cheerleading is fun of course, but it's not enough to keep a person waking up every day saying, "Oh my gosh! I am the luckiest person alive because I am a cheerleader! I now feel happy and I will continue to be happy all day long!" No, that is a little ditsy and you probably recognize that, but I wonder: When you think of what will make you happy, are you

able to distinguish your crazy thought patterns? It is always hard to think clearly about your own life concerning these things. Try something. Write down ten things that you believe will make you happy on the list below. Start each with *"I would be happy if . . ."*

1.
2.
3.
4.
5.
6.
7.
8.
9.
10.

Now look over the list and honestly assess whether there is any difference from my ditsy cheerleader quote regarding anything on your list. Granted, your list might be more other's centered. Maybe you wrote down, "I would be happy if my grandma weren't sick with cancer." Or maybe, "I would be happy if

IS POPULARITY THE ANSWER TO HAPPINESS?

THE WORLD'S HAPPY COMES AND GOES BUT PEACE AND JOY IS SOMETHING THAT NO PERSON CAN TAKE AWAY FROM YOU.

my parents were back together." And I gotta give it to you—those types of wishes are much deeper and more thoughtful than making cheerleader or getting a unending credit line at Sephora, but . . . so many of our "happy" requests are about getting out from under the discomfort in our lives. And about believing lies.

For example, making cheerleader is often perceived as achieving popularity and acceptance. So that would mean if you make cheerleader, then there is no more discomfort wondering if you've arrived on the social scene—right? Wrong. You and I both know plenty of insecure cheerleaders. What about being

happy if your grandma's cancer goes away? Well, it is very rational to believe that would make you (and a lot of other people) happy, but we also need to look into the comfort vs. discomfort issue I mentioned. Honestly, God is not all about our happiness, but he is all about our well-being and sometimes the two can seem very different from a personal point of view. Here's what I mean . . .

When I was in middle school, I witnessed a murder that I felt crashed and ruined my life. I was not happy about it and wanted God to make all the repercussions of the incident go away. I didn't want to see the mental pictures, I didn't want to feel afraid, and I didn't want to have to forgive the person who did it. If I could have prayed for one important thing to be happy, I would have requested a rewind from God. I would have asked him to take me out of the classroom where the murder took place or, better yet, just erase the murder all together. For many years I felt that would have fixed the problem. But as I got older and dealt with the discomfort in my life and after I got over thinking that I had been treated unfairly because I was there in the room, I started realizing I could have some deep down God happy—peace and joy is what the Bible calls it—in spite of all other circumstances.* That grasp of deep down God happy is what I really needed because there is a truth to be understood about the world's version of "happy." It is fleeting. The world's happy comes and goes, but peace and joy is something that no person or circumstance can take away from you. Your grandma's cancer can't take peace and joy away. Your parents' divorce can't take peace and joy away.

Romans 15:13 says it this way, "May the God of hope fill you with all joy and peace as you trust in him, so that you may overflow with hope by the power of the Holy Spirit" (jer).

The secret to a happy life is placing your "happy" in God and God's hope for your life. When you are able to trust God and believe that he has your best interest in mind, you will experience the deep down God happy. Does that mean you will never experience disappointments? Gut-wrenching hardships? Confusing personal relationships? Serious and stunning situations? Of course not. We all will have our share of these kinds of issues in life—it's inevitable. Jesus not only predicted problems in our life, he warned about them. And our refusal to be realistic about this, hanging on to the world's idea of happiness, positions us to believe a lie about life.

Look at the words of Jesus in John 16:33, "I have told you all this so that you may have peace in me. Here on earth you will have many trials and sorrows. But take heart, because I have overcome the world" (jhp). Jesus the realist. So the truth is there will be unhappy stuff that happens which will bring discomfort into our lives and we can't control that, but God has promised to care for us in those situations, giving us peace and joy despite any

OH !! SUCH JOY

circumstances. So my wish for you and for me is a continuing deep belief in God.

How Will I Know if the Path I Am Taking Is the One God Has for Me or if It's the Wrong One?

Searching for God's will in your life is the ongoing struggle for many Christians. Wouldn't it be great if God gave us a road map so we could make sure and never go wrong? The truth is that he has given us a road map in the Bible though it is likely not as well-defined as we would like it. You won't flip open the Bible to find who you are supposed to date or marry. You won't find out specifics on what college you are supposed to attend or what to major in. And you probably already know that you won't find God's perfect will for your life about whether or not you should cut bangs!

However, God does have ideas about what he desires for your life and mine. For one, John 6:40 says, "For my Father's will is that everyone who looks to the Son and believes in him shall have eternal life" (jer). And another piece of God's will includes 1 Thessalonians 4:3 which says, "It is God's will that you should be sanctified" (jer).

THE SECRET TO A HAPPY LIFE IS PLACING YOUR "HAPPY" IN GOD AND GOD'S HOPE FOR YOUR LIFE.

SO THE BEST ADVICE FOR STAYING ON THE RIGHT PATH IS STAYING CLOSE TO GOD AND HIS WORD.

We can know with certainty that God's will for you and me is that we would become Christians and grow in our faith. Those are givens, so I am thinking that is not exactly what you are wondering about.

You are probably wondering about getting off on the wrong path dating the wrong person. Or maybe taking the wrong job. Or signing up for the wrong classes. Maybe there is a choice about whether or not to go to a party or to go on a trip. There are millions of everyday choices and it sounds like you want to make sure to make the right choices where God is concerned. I have to tell you that it says a lot about your heart for thinking that way. I imagine God is proud of you for desiring to please him. He is our Father and just like any good daddy, he is proud of his kids when their heart is in the right place. I hope knowing that makes you feel good.

Although there are no one, two, three steps to determining God's path for your life, there are some basic guidelines to put you on the path to making good decisions. God gave us his Word to help us in our daily life. He left us with verses from the Bible about loving him and honoring him first and letting the directions for our individual life spill out of our love and devotion. Jeremiah 6:16 says, "So now the Lᴋɴ' says, 'Stop right where you are! Look for the old, godly way, and walk in it. Travel its path, and you will find rest for your souls'" (jhp). This "old, godly way" is found in the pages of the Bible. So the best advice for staying on the right path is staying close to God and his Word. When we actively love God and his Word, then our thinking produces stable, right thinking that the Bible calls wisdom. And when we apply wisdom in our actions and decisions, we stay on the right path. Romans 12:2 says it like this, "Don't copy the behavior and customs of this world, but let God transform you into a new person by changing the way you think. Then you will know what God wants you to do, and you will know how good and pleasing and perfect his will really is" (jhp).

And I know this sounds incredibly simplistic and vague, but it is the answer God provided in the Bible. What is the best way to ensure you know God's path for your life? Saturate your mind in the Bible; soak up biblical teaching; hang around people who wholeheartedly love God; be willing to wait on things when you are unsure of yourself; and pray like crazy to have the understanding to make decisions that will honor God in your life.

* For more on dealing with painful situations, check out the article, "The Small Answer to the Big Question: Why Do Bad Things Happen?" on page 88.

weigh in @ virtuous reality .com

LOVIN' GOD'S WORD!

Q's ABOUT GUYS

$\mathcal{Pearls}$ and PIGS

by Vicki Courtney

With the rise in popularity of social networking sites like MySpace and Facebook, many teens type things they would never in a million years say to someone's face. Chances are you have experienced the awkwardness of having a guy say something to you that is sexually inappropriate.

I am shocked to see some of the comments posted by guys on Christian girls' pages. While I am disappointed in the guys, I can't help but wonder why these girls allow the guys to talk inappropriately to them. Are they so desperate for attention that they are willing to settle for the wrong kind of attention? I can't help but think that some of these girls are even flattered by the comments or they would have removed them from their page. One such Christian girl, who listed the Bible as a favorite book, had numerous sexually inappropriate comments posted on her page. One guy friend jokingly described in graphic detail a sexual act he wanted to perform on her. I know, I know, it's all in jest. But it's not funny.

Some guys will test a girl's limits to see if they will tolerate sexual banter. It's similar to what happens

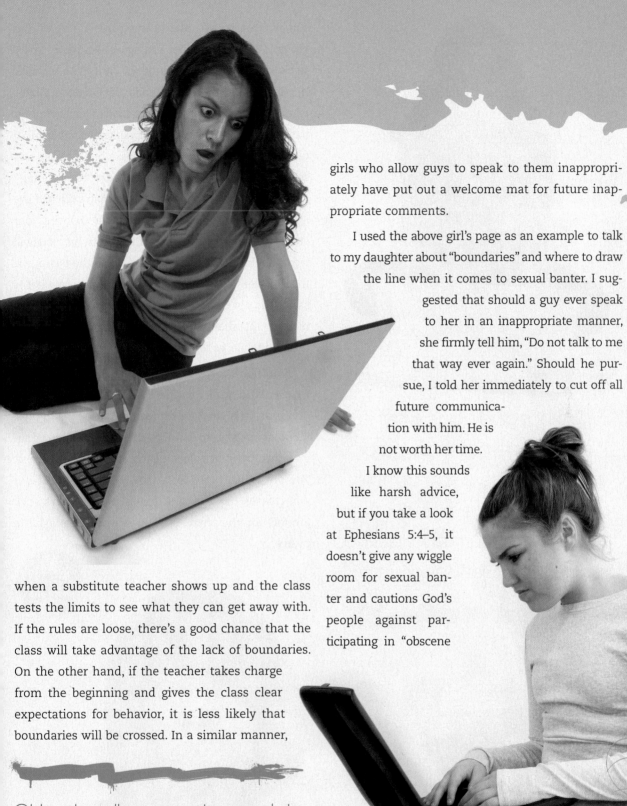

girls who allow guys to speak to them inappropriately have put out a welcome mat for future inappropriate comments.

I used the above girl's page as an example to talk to my daughter about "boundaries" and where to draw the line when it comes to sexual banter. I suggested that should a guy ever speak to her in an inappropriate manner, she firmly tell him, "Do not talk to me that way ever again." Should he pursue, I told her immediately to cut off all future communication with him. He is not worth her time.

I know this sounds like harsh advice, but if you take a look at Ephesians 5:4–5, it doesn't give any wiggle room for sexual banter and cautions God's people against participating in "obscene

when a substitute teacher shows up and the class tests the limits to see what they can get away with. If the rules are loose, there's a good chance that the class will take advantage of the lack of boundaries. On the other hand, if the teacher takes charge from the beginning and gives the class clear expectations for behavior, it is less likely that boundaries will be crossed. In a similar manner,

Girls who allow guys to speak to them inappropriately have put out a welcome mat for future inappropriate comments.

"Do not give dogs what is sacred; do not throw your pearls to pigs. If you do, they may trample them under their feet, and then turn and tear you to pieces" (Matthew 7:6 NIV).

stories, foolish talk, and coarse jokes" (NLT). It also brought to mind another passage of Scripture where Jesus was preaching to the crowd on a mountainside. It starts in Matthew 5 and ends three chapters later. I know that you are probably not fond of long sermons, but this one is well worth reading in your spare time. In fact, Matthew 7:28 says, "When Jesus had finished this sermon, the crowds were astonished at his teaching". Consider it a sort of pep talk on how to live life and live it to the fullest. He covered everything from loving your enemies (ouch) to not obsessing over what you will wear (double ouch). But tucked away in the passage is this priceless bit of advice: "Do not give dogs what is sacred; do not throw your pearls to pigs. If you do, they may trample them under their feet, and then turn and tear you to pieces" (Matthew 7:6).

You don't have to search long on MySpace and Facebook to find countless examples of insecure Christian girls who are throwing their pearls to pigs. Slopping in the mud with the swine rather than guarding their priceless pearls in a treasure chest. You are worth more than that. Remember that if a guy crosses the line with sexual banter, don't stick around for the mud bath. Save your pearls for a prince. ★

weigh in
@
virtuous
reality
.com

Will the Real Mr. Right
PLEASE STAND UP?

I remember it as if it were yesterday. Dancing in the arms of my boyfriend at his cousin's wedding, it felt so right. Surely this was the man I was meant to spend the rest of my life with. I had never thought much about marriage before then. Sure, like most other girls, I dreamed of the day I would meet my Prince Charming, but up until that moment, none of the candidates had left me wanting to pick up a copy of Modern Bride at the checkout stand. Maybe the wedding I was attending had rubbed off on me and left me with the marriage bug. I was twenty years old at the time and we had dated for nearly a year. Everyone said we were perfect together. But everything wasn't always as perfect as it looked from the outside. What they didn't know was that he was extremely jealous and did not like me talking much to other guys, including my guy friends. Sometimes I felt smothered in the relationship, but I always justified that he must really care or he wouldn't be so jealous and possessive. None of that mattered on this night. As the song came to an end, he whispered softly in my ear, "I want to marry you. I wish this was our wedding." Funny, I was thinking the same thing at that moment. With my eyes closed and my head on his shoulder, I imagined that I was the lucky bride dancing in the arms of her groom. They say you'll know when its right, and it felt so right. A few days after the wedding, he showed up with a dozen roses and a card. In the card he wrote, "This card can be exchanged for an engagement ring. I love you."

Today, I still have the card, but no ring to show

BEFORE, i FELT LIKE i CARRiED THE BURDEN FOR FiGURiNG OUT THE WHOLE MR. RiGHT THiNG ON MY OWN. NOW, i HAVE GOD TO DiRECT MY STEPS.

for it.

Fortunately, I wised up and ended the relationship in the months that followed. This guy couldn't have been more wrong for me. I learned a lot of lessons in that relationship, like:

- 💜 *jealousy and possessiveness* are a flag that something is wrong . . . not a sign that things are right.
- 💜 *if fighting is common* in the relationship, a promise of marriage, engagement ring, or a wedding will not make it go away.
- 💜 *emotions cannot be relied upon* when it comes to determining Mr. Right. Oftentimes your heart will say "yes" while the facts surrounding the relationship say "no."

I still find it disturbing that I almost headed down the path of marrying this guy. Every now and then, I find myself thinking about how disastrous that mistake would have been. I have met plenty of women who are living out the consequences of marrying

Mr. Wrong. Of course, none of them set out to marry Mr. Wrong and obviously, at some point, the guy seemed like Mr. Right or they probably wouldn't have said, "I do."

I ended up meeting the real Mr. Right about a year after my break up with Mr. Wrong. A friend invited me to a Christian conference for college students, and it was there that I met my future husband. But even more exciting than that, I met the real love of my life—Jesus Christ. When I became a Christian, my standards for a future husband changed. Before, I felt like I carried the burden for figuring out the whole Mr. Right thing on my own. Now, I had God to direct my steps. I actually told my friend at the retreat that, "I'm going to marry that Keith guy." We didn't immediately begin dating, which is a good thing, because I needed to focus first and foremost on my new relationship with Christ. I had a major "secret" crush on him for months, but I trusted God with the details. He even asked out one of my friends during that time! Ugh. Finally, I told God one morning in my prayer time, "I don't want Keith Courtney if you don't want him for me." Would you believe that later that day, I stumbled upon a quote in a book I was reading and it said this: "God's delays are not God's denials." I wrote it on a slip of notebook paper and hung it on my refrigerator in my kitchen. Every time I saw it, I felt like it was God's personal word of encouragement for me to hang in there. It was our little secret. About a month later, Keith and I were hanging out as friends and he confessed that he was beginning to like me for "more than a friend." I wanted to say, "Duh, what took you so long?!" Eight months later, he proposed—exactly one year since meeting him at the retreat. Nine months after that, we were married. Today, we have been married for twenty years and we are more in love today than we were on the day we walked down the aisle and said, "I do."

There is nothing wrong with dreaming about the day you will meet your Mr. Right and get married. In fact, out of the more than four hundred girls who answered our survey question, "If you could ask God one question and get an immediate answer, what would you ask?," the second most common question girls in the survey said

Who Will I Marry?

they would ask God is, "Who will I marry?" Many of you realize that marriage will probably be one of the most important events in your life. Some of you come from divorced homes and you desperately want to avoid the pain of divorce in your own marriage. Even though many of you are young and marriage may not be on your radar just yet, it's still important to think about your standards for a guy— even if you have not yet begun to date.

Which brings us to the million dollar question: "How then can a girl be certain when the time comes that she has chosen the real 'Mr. Right' and they will go

GOD'S DELAYS ARE NOT DENIALS.

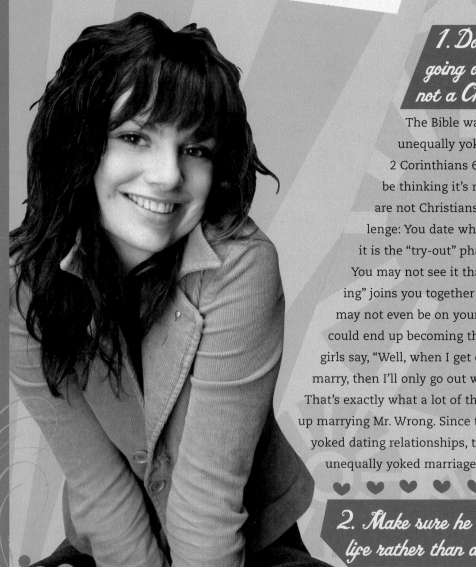

MARRIAGE MAY NOT EVEN BE ON YOUR RADAR, BUT ANY GUY YOU DATE COULD END UP BECOMING THE MAN YOU MARRY.

on to live happily ever after?" She can't. I know that's probably not the answer you want to hear, but because we are a sinful people, there are no guarantees when it comes to predicting the success of a marriage. There are, however, certain factors that greatly increase your odds of marrying a Mr. Right—and remaining married to him.

1. Do not even think about going out with a guy who is not a Christian. ♥ ♥ ♥ ♥

The Bible warns against believers being unequally yoked with unbelievers (see 2 Corinthians 6:14). I know some of you may be thinking it's no big deal to date guys who are not Christians, but let me give you this challenge: You date who you marry. When you date, it is the "try-out" phase that precedes marriage. You may not see it that way, but the truth is, "dating" joins you together with another person. Marriage may not even be on your radar, but any guy you date could end up becoming the man you marry. I have heard girls say, "Well, when I get closer to the age where I might marry, then I'll only go out with Christian guys." Yeah, sure. That's exactly what a lot of the women said who ended up marrying Mr. Wrong. Since they had justified unequally yoked dating relationships, they found it easy to justify an unequally yoked marriage . . . until the problems set in.

♥ ♥ ♥ ♥ ♥

2. Make sure he leads a "God-directed" life rather than a "self-directed" life.

Someone who is living a God-directed life is in the habit of yielding to God. Just like when you are driving and you see a yield sign, it warns you to slow down and give cars in your path the right-of-way. A guy that slows down when making decisions and gives God the right-of-way is in the habit of yielding all areas of his life to God. When difficulties arise in marriage (and they will), he will do what he has always done . . . yield to God.

3. Pray for your future husband.

Pray that he will grow in wisdom and knowledge of God's truths. Pray that he is in the process of becoming the spiritual leader that God desires him to be. Pray that God will help him to guard his heart and his purity. If he has stumbled in regard to his purity, pray that he has experienced conviction, remorse for his actions, and a change in his behavior.

Of course, this all assumes that you are deserving of such a guy. If you want to end up with Mr. Right, make sure you are striving to become Miss Right. It is never too early to work on becoming Miss Right. Miss Right is first and foremost "right with her God," and that begins today. Are you a Christian? I never want to assume that everyone reading this is a Christian, so if you're not quite sure, be sure to read "A Leap of Faith" on page 84 and "The Scoop on . . . Heaven" on page 92. Do you live a God-directed life? Are you in the habit of yielding to God? Will you refuse to date guys who aren't Christians? What about solid Christians? For those of you who haven't begun dating, it's best if you can start off with God's standards. Be picky. Remember, dating is a practice field for marriage. If you set the bar high from the very beginning, chances are, it will remain high when the stakes are high. You just never know when you'll meet your Mr. Right. Or maybe . . . you've met him already. Hopefully, it's not that annoying guy on your bus who can belch to the tune of the song on the radio and make tooting noises with his armpits. But, you just never know . . . ✱

IT IS NEVER TOO EARLY TO WORK ON BECOMING MISS RIGHT.

QUIZ:

Are you dateable?

by Susie Davis

Are you dateable? Well, yes of course you are . . . but to whom? That's the real question. If you are always attracting "the wrong kind of guy," there might be a reason for it. Take this short quiz to sort out the kind of guys you are attracting.

1. Right before a history exam, a cute guy whispers to you that he didn't have a chance to study and asks you if he can glance at your paper for answers. You:

a) move your arm to keep from blocking his view of your test, hoping this will seal the deal for a homecoming date.

b) move your arm to block his view of your test and consider that the end of your crush.

2. You overhear a guy in the hall say he wants to be careful about dating because he is trying to honor God. You:

a) look at him and shake your head as if he just said he believes in aliens.

b) look at him and shake your head in disbelief that there are still godly guys in your school.

3. The quarterback of the football team makes a crude joke in front of you. You:

a) smile, shrug your shoulders, and laughing, stay put. You don't want to walk away and look like a dork.

b) smile, shrug your shoulders, and walk away. You don't want to listen to that stuff.

4. A new guy at school sits down at lunch next to you and says, "Hey, what's God teaching you lately?" You:

a) silently wonder if God is teaching his algebra class or something.

b) remain silent, feeling shy because you have never had a guy ask about your spiritual life.

5. A great looking guy walks up to talk to you in the hall, and you notice he keeps looking you over while he is talking without actually looking at your face. You:

a) consider his long look a compliment and hope that means he'll look you over as you walk away too.

b) consider his long look proof of a serious lack of self-control and a character flaw and find a way to escape in the crowd.

6. You are headed to the cafeteria for lunch and just as you turn the corner, a guy quickly moves to open the door for you and your friends. You:

a) look him in the face, roll your eyes, and shuffle on through the door with your friends.

b) look him in the face, thank him sincerely, and walk graciously through the door.

7. There is a girl in your computer class who is handicapped and has trouble with the assignments. A super popular guy in the class mimics her behind her back. You:

a) tell him he's so funny and hope he'll pay more attention to you in the future.

b) tell him to cut it out and hope he'll leave her alone in the future.

8. You are on a date with a guy you have a huge crush on. After dinner he suggests taking you back to his house because his parents are gone. You:

a) think carefully about creating a believable excuse for your parents since you will be later than expected after going to his house.

b) think carefully about whether you should call your mom or dad to pick you up ASAP at the restaurant from this dead-end date.

9. A cute guy you just met asks to give you a ride home from school. While getting in the car, you notice a half empty bottle of Tequila on the floor of the back seat. You:

a) tell yourself that someone else probably left it in the car and this cutie doesn't even know about it.

b) tell yourself that you have no intention of getting in the car with him, excuse yourself, smile, and head to the opposite end of the parking lot.

10. You are standing in the parking lot at work talking to a guy you think is pretty good looking. While you are talking he takes a call on his cell and during the conversation he starts cussing—a lot. You:

a) motion to him that you'll wait while he finishes up with his call.

b) motion to him that you need to leave and forget about liking that guy.

11. Your date to the prom shows up at your house, and when you start down the stairs, you notice he is sitting and talking to your parents and your little brother, laughing and having a good time. You:

a) wait for a minute longer wondering what in the world he could possibly have to talk about with your parents and your little brother that would be interesting at all.

b) wait for a minute longer wondering how you managed to get such a respectful guy to take you to the prom.

If you got . . .

MOSTLY A: If you scored mostly "A," then you are attracting guys that might be more Mr. Wrong than Mr. Right. Consider that many of your actions are a reflection of your heart, and in this case your heart looks pretty consumed with attracting a guy no matter his standards.

If you want a respectable guy, you might think about how you are responding to guys in general and kick it up a notch. Pray and ask God for help in this area with guys or ask your friends to hold you accountable on some of your less than stellar behavior. You don't have to get crazy just because a boy is around. Stand up for what you believe in, and then you'll make better decisions about the guys you want to be around.

MOSTLY B: If you scored mostly "B," then you are headed in the right direction, leading you to a potential Mr. Right. Your decisions are based on your beliefs and a deep-rooted sense of your identity in God. This is all good news so keep up the great work! Keep on following your intuition and good common sense, and you might just find the kind of guy girls dream about . . . a guy who loves God as much as you do. ✱

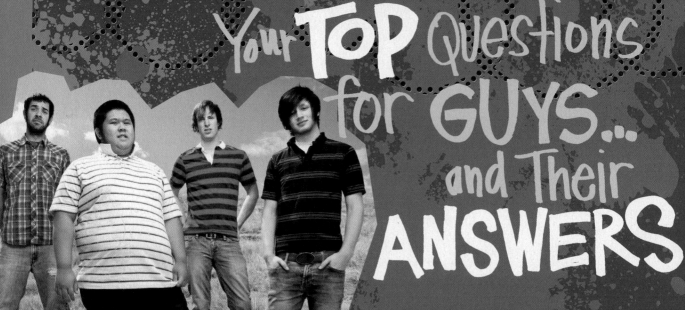

Your TOP Questions for GUYS... and Their ANSWERS.

by Vicki Courtney

In our survey we gave girls your age an opportunity to ask guys the one question that's burning on their hearts. More than four hundred girls took the time to let us know. We compiled a list of the most commonly asked questions, and a few interesting ones to boot, and turned them over to a guy panel of more than forty guys. We asked each guy to answer the questions and what you will find here is only a sampling of their answers. Before you jump in and read what they had to say, I want you to remember a few things. First of all, while most of the guys we surveyed are Christian guys, this does not in any way mean that we agree 100 percent with their comments and endorse their answers as acceptable. As you will see, the guys were candidly honest and rather than print only the answers that would make Jesus smile, we wanted to give you a realistic cross section of what the average Christian guy is thinking. That said, we edited very little; and at times you might find that they use a word or make a statement that sounds harsh. Again, we do not endorse everything they say, but we did not want to bring you manufactured results or answers that we "prettied up." Some of their answers are endearing, some are blunt, and at times, some are offensive. Again, they offer girls a unique glimpse of what is running through their minds when it comes to girls.

By printing their answers to your questions, we hope you will be left with a better understanding of the male mind. We also hope that you will see the dangers of stereotyping guys into categories. When addressing guy issues in the TeenVirtue series, we try to be "guy advocates." It is not our desire to participate in the "male-bashing" that we often see in today's culture that is quick to stereotype guys as insensitive individuals. By printing their honest answers, you will see that some are sensitive and think deeply. Others are more spontaneous and say the first thing that pops into their minds. Yet others are witty and blunt. Some are obviously more mature in the faith than others, but we can't expect them all to be missionaries-in-training. They are not perfect, but neither are we. In the end, you'll see that much can be learned from their answers. What you choose to do with the information will be up to you.

1. Describe the perfect girl.

Beautiful, caring, smart, and she smells nice. — Josh, 14

Christian, confident, talkative, good cook, amazing video game skills, strange obsession with all the sports teams I like. — Ryan, 18

Beauty is a bonus. I think Jesus gives Christian guys eyes to see inner beauty. With that said, I would love a girl who has the same interests as I do, follows Christ, is funny, helps those in need and is not stuck on herself. — Geoff, 15

Christian, smart, not overly needy/high maintenance, active, funny but able to have serious conversations, generally happy, and able to help me through anything. — Travis, 16

She has to have a great personality. She has to be able to carry on the most intellectual conversations and the absolute dumbest ones, as well. She would have to be in love with sports like me because that's basically all I think about. — Jared, 16

For me, I look a lot at 1 Corinthians 13 and Proverbs 31 for qualities that make up the perfect girl. She needs to be living for Jesus and willing to choose Jesus over a guy. She should be open and honest and there needs to be a tad bit of randomness there as well. Dressing modestly is also huge. — Jake, 16

The perfect girl has confidence and integrity. She has total reliance on God in his wisdom, truth, and power. Christian morals are very important in her life. Just her love for Jesus Christ makes her so attractive. — Clint, 18

There has to be physical attraction as well as personality attraction, if that makes sense. She needs to be well-mannered and nice and not dress like a slut. — Tom, 16

She needs to go to church, read God's Word, and pray. She needs to have a sense of humor. She needs to be someone I can share my problems with and who will share hers with me. — Nathan, 14

Understanding, forgiving, tender, loving, and nurturing. Likes to snuggle but won't tell your

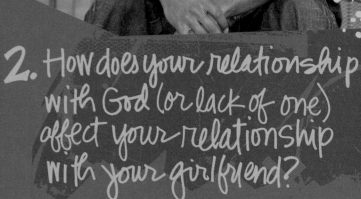

guy friends you like to! She understands your need to be macho sometimes. She doesn't pressure you. Brunette. — Matt, 18

Nice, somebody you can have fun with but still bring home to Mom. She can cook and is in shape. — Spencer, 14

A girl who honors God first in all things, including her parents. In love with God first and always. Funny, outgoing, musical, encouraging, and has a heart for people and doing God's work. — Ben, 17

She is definitely a Christian. Beautiful, positive attitude, isn't fake, and loves Christ more than anything. — Logan, 16

Christian, not too outgoing, sweet, sympathetic, modest, and doesn't care too much about what others think. — Jerrod, 18

Well, I guess the perfect girl is someone who laughs at my jokes, even the dumb ones. She isn't overweight and is comfortable with who she is. She wants a relationship with God and sticks to her convictions. — Chris, 16

She boldly seeks after the Lord despite what her peers think of her. She has integrity, honesty, is trustworthy, patient, uncompromising in her beliefs, confident in herself, and has an outward beauty that is only made complete by the inner qualities above. — Matt, 16

Long flowing brown hair, curls preferably, lives in Texas, loves God more than she loves me. — Veston, 15

She is a Christian, smart, pretty good-looking, good personality, virgin, independent, treats her parents good, semi-athletic. — Cabe, 14

2. How does your relationship with God (or lack of one) affect your relationship with your girlfriend?

I need to have a solid relationship with God before having a girlfriend. The hope is that I would help my girlfriend grow closer to God and vice versa. God should never come second to a girlfriend in my opinion. — Travis, 16

She is to be a Christian or at least go to church before I will go out with her. — Jared, 16

When I've kind of fallen away from God, it's really hard for me to encourage my girlfriend in a godly way. In the same way though, when my relationship with God is going good, it's a lot easier for me to encourage her from a biblical standpoint and pray for her. — Jake, 16

My relationship with God teaches me to have kindness, patience, and respect toward my girlfriend. I strive to not envy, not boast, or keep a record

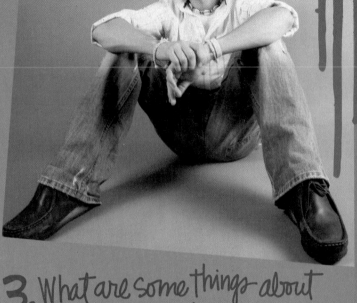

of wrongs. With God, I always protect, always trust, and always hope for the best for my girlfriend. It helps me stay true to God's Word and remain pure for that special day when I get married. — Clint, 18

My relationship with God helps me remember what is important and helps me to return to the right path whenever I make a mistake and stray. I know that I will always be forgiven, so when I fail I don't despair, but I also don't give up trying. — Matt, 18

My relationship with God affects how I treat my girlfriend, how I look at her, and how we act together. The point of the relationship is to help each other grow in our relationship with Christ before our relationship with each other. — Ben, 17

Well, I just told my girlfriend that I was breaking up because it was affecting my relationship with God, soooo . . . — Remick, 16

I don't have a girlfriend so thanks for bringing up a painful subject! — Joe, 15

I don't currently have a girlfriend, but I was in a relationship for over a year and can say that you should stay away from too much one-on-one time because that leads to too much temptation. — Matt, 16

3. What are some things about girls that send you running in the opposite direction?

DRAMA, shy, insecure, gossipers, forwardness, too flirty. — Ryan, 18

Incredibly self-conscious girls who care so much about how they look that they aren't able to be themselves. — John, 16

Smoking, drinking, swearing constantly, overly competitive, rude/mean to people, suggestive/immodest clothing, overly dramatic, blows things out of proportion. — Travis, 16

Dressing inappropriately or pushing the dress code rules, especially at church. For example, I just went on a mission trip and some of the girls were obsessing over rolling up their T-shirt sleeves and pant legs so they wouldn't get weird tan lines. If you truly want a godly guy, he's not going to care about your tan lines, and he's probably not going to be interested unless you put on more clothes. — Will, 15

A ditz. Guys don't buy that front. We know girls are smarter than that and the fact that they choose to act stupid or unintelligent is a total turn off. — Ben, 17

The goose laugh! (Just kidding.) Seriously, the kind of girls that never leave you alone—really pushy girls! — Landon, 14

Bad attitude. If a girl is real snobby and thinks she's better than everyone else, it's really annoying. Also, if she has no manners and acts just like one of the guys. — Tom, 16

Overly flirtatious, being easy, lack of self-respect, mean to other girls, into drugs and alcohol, aggressive, overly sexual. — Matt, 18

If they always need to be in the limelight—the ones who talk about themselves all the time. — Riley, 15

Cussing, drug use, skanky clothing, and a bad attitude. — Logan, 16

Loud, obnoxious, show off, boastful, and critical of others. — Jarrod, 18

When they wear so much makeup! They are beautiful no matter what. — Holden, 15

The way many of them dress can send me running. Loud, boasting, and gossipy nature instead of a gentle and quiet spirit like the Bible talks about. — Matt, 16

Smoking, bad manners, bad teeth,

bad hygiene, not modest, whiney, two-faced, treats grown-ups bad (teachers, parents, etc.). — Cabe, 14

Acting dumb when they aren't; talks too much. — Matthew, 16

When girls are really flashy in a sexual way. I know they're just trying to get attention and that's not what I'm looking for. — Nicholas, 14

4. What actions or aspects about girls cause you to stumble the most in your walk with Christ?

Dressing inappropriately. — Travis, 16

When really cute girls are touchy feely, it can throw you off spiritually. Sometimes, one thing leads to another. — Will, 15

The way some girls dress or how they talk (crudeness and stuff). — Benjamin, 17

When they dress in real skimpy clothes. It's a real temptation to look. — Tom, 16

To be honest, it's very hard for a guy to restrain himself in a sexually tempting situation, and it does not make it easy if the girl is willing. To stay pure, both the guy and the girl have to work together. — Matt, 18

Tight clothes. Ugh, they drive me insane. Here I am trying to be a good guy that a girl can rely on and BOOM, a girl walks by with everything right there. It's hard to keep a pure mind when you see more than anyone needs to see. — Ben, 17

Lack of clothing. — Matt, 17

The way many of them dress, particularly low-cut shirts. Girls, I understand that you are under a ridiculous amount of pressure to look a certain way, but please strive for modesty to help your Christian brothers out! We will do our part to look you in the eyes when we are talking to you rather than at your chest! — Matt, 16

5. Is sex usually the main thing on a a guy's mind?

76.4 percent of the time. — Ryan, 18

There's a good chance. — John, 16

Not all the time. — Will, 15

I can't speak for all guys, but for me, no. — Benjamin, 17

It depends. If I'm watching a soccer game, no. Other times, yes. — Matt, 18

If not the main thing, it's high up on the list. — Spencer, 14

Not for me, but for most other guys. — Kevin, 17

It's always there, but it's not always the main focus. — Andrew, 17

No, and it's really insulting when people say that. — Chris, 16

6. What do you think when you see a girl dressed inappropriately?

Bless her heart. She must feel like she has to dress that way to get attention. — Ryan, 18

Sometimes I let my guard down and think something I shouldn't. I try to glorify Jesus with pure eyes and pure thoughts. — Geoff, 15

They need to respect themselves and everyone else around them by dressing more modestly. — Travis, 16

Do you want my sweatshirt? I really struggle with lust, so when girls dress inappropriately, it's really hard on me. Especially, when I'm in a classroom and can't escape from the temptation. — Jake, 16

I think that the girl is convinced that it's the only way she can get attention. It makes me think she's not self-confident and that she's easy. — Tom, 16

I think she probably doesn't have the best relationship with God, she probably isn't that smart, and she needs guys to look at her, which has a whole different set of meanings attached to it. If she's pretty, it's hard not to look. I'm not perfect. I try not to linger and let my thoughts progress to lust. — Matt, 18

My heart says, "Look out!" My mind says, "Oh yeah!" — Trevor, 14

My first reaction is, "Wow." But then the Holy Spirit is like, "Dude, what are you doing?!" These girls are giving way too much of themselves away to the world. — Ben, 17

I think that if they really felt like they were pretty, they wouldn't have to dress that way. They have no respect for themselves or their parents. — Mario, 14

I think they are desperate. — Alex, 15

I wonder if her parents have any control over her. — Landon, 14

Sex. — Joe, 15

Well, sometimes I want to look, but eventually I realize that they aren't the kind of girls I want to be with. — Chris, 16

Where are her parents? — Daniel, 16

I think that she doesn't have good parents and needs attention. — Cabe, 14

7. *Why do some guys act like they like you one day and then completely ignore you the next?*

I think you are over-analyzing this . . . we are really very simple. — Ryan, 18

We're probably having a bad day or stressed about something. —Noah, 14

Guys have bad days just like girls and sometimes we just feel like ignoring people. —Jared, 16

Guys don't even know they're doing it. In all honesty, we have no clue that you like us and we have no clue that we are tearing up your heart by the way we act. — Jake, 16

Probably because guys are always trying to impress others. —Colton, 15

The world may never know . . . —Tom, 16

Here's what I think: most commonly, they don't know they are "acting like they like you" and more than likely, they're just good friends with you and have no further intentions; less commonly, they like you and are too embarrassed or don't know how to go about telling you or asking you out; they like you, but around certain people, it's more important that they be "cool" than like you. — Matt, 18

Depends on the guy. Some like you but don't think you like them, and they don't want to be vulnerable, so they act like they don't like you anymore. And some are just so shallow that they change every other day to the girl they think is the easiest or hottest or whatever. — Jarrod, 18

Sometimes our guy friends talk us out of liking the girl. — Landon, 14

Maybe he's decided he doesn't have a chance. — Joe, 15

Either because they are fickle in their relationships or they are not sure if it's God's will for them to be in a relationship at that time. — Matt, 16

Because some guys hang around with their friends too much and their friends may give them the wrong impression of you. They decide to believe their friends and start ignoring you. — Veston, 15

Sometimes, I will have these short love spells that I know don't mean anything so I will flirt and hang out with a girl. Then after going home and talking with my man friends, I realize she is not a girl that fits my standards. — Nicholas, 14

8. Would you rather spend a day talking to a girl you like or an hour kissing her?

This is the dumbest question I have ever heard. I don't function on a schedule like this and I am not sure of any guy who does. — Ryan, 18

Well, a day talking with a few kisses thrown in. — Jacob, 17

Depends. If she talks about boring stuff, but she is a good kisser . . . — Tom, 16

That's a tough question. Kissing probably. — Trevor, 14

Half and half. — Spencer, 14

Talking would be better. Kissing only lasts a few seconds but words can last a lifetime. — Ben, 17

Talking because kissing will get you nothing but trouble. — Logan, 16

I would rather talk. — Landon, 14

Definitely, talking. — Cabe, 14

9. What kind of things do guys talk about when you're alone with your guy friends? Do you talk about girls at all?

Sports (82 percent), video games (17.8 percent), girls (0.2 percent). For example, I didn't even know one of my closest friends had broken up with his girlfriend until about two months after it happened. —Ryan, 18

Mainly sports, games, what's happening in the church, and sometimes girls. — Noah, 14

We talk about whatever is on our mind. A lot of times it is about sports or some sort of game. Guys talk about girls for brief moments, but not like whole conversations that last two hours. — Travis, 16

We talk about sports, girls, and stupid stuff. Anything really that comes to mind. — Will, 15

When I'm around my friends that don't have Christ-centered lives, they talk about the new hottest girl, who has a hotter girlfriend, who is hot right now, basically, it's who is hot. It's disgusting and perverted like who has a nice butt or rack. I don't talk like this, but I'm just being honest about other guys who don't respect girls. When I'm with my friends from church, we usually talk about a cool trick we did on our bike, how we jumped off a bridge or blew something up. When we talk about girls, it's usually about how some girls need to cover up more. It's more of a discussion about concern for a certain girl or group of girls. — Jake, 16

Yeah, sometimes we talk about girls but mostly we just make fun of each other. — Carter, 17

Occasionally, but not as much as girls talk about guys. — Tom, 16

Sometimes we talk about girls, but most of the time we talk about video games. — Nathan 14

Girls, sports players who are great and some who are overrated, and how the teams we like are doing. — Spencer, 14

Depends on the guys, but girls always pop up somewhere in the conversation. Sometimes guys will talk locker-room talk and some guys (not me and my friends) talk about who is having sex with who and who they are gonna "do" next. Just being honest, here. — Ben, 17

We talk about two things: sports and girls. — Mario, 14

We talk about girls, but not as much as they probably think. We pretty much talk about stupid stuff. — Remick, 16

Movies and sports mostly, sometimes about the Bible, and sometimes about girls. — Matt, 16

Cars, movies, music, sound systems. Girls, some. — Matthew, 16

When guys are alone they talk about a lot of things, especially in small groups at church. We talk about our mission to purity and bug each other about the girl a guy likes, and who would be a good girl to like. And then there's politics, pranks, and fireworks. You get the picture. — Nicholas, 14

10. How can we tell if a guy likes us for a friend or something more?

Ask him. — Ryan, 18

If we flirt with you or pester you—but not like in kindergarten where we chased you around the playground and tried to tackle you. — Hayden, 14

As a gentleman, I try to be courteous to all women. If I liked a girl as more than a friend, I would probably try to spend time alone with that girl whether at church or in a group, so I can get to know her better. — Geoff, 15

If we are trying to hang around you, nicer to you than the other girls, and if we are doing anything to get a hug. — Will, 15

Sometimes, it's hard to tell and most of the time the guy doesn't even know, himself. — Jacob, 17

If it were me, I would just tell you straight out. — Carter, 17

A guy likes you as a friend if he is nice and respects your wishes. If a guy likes you for something more, he's usually more affectionate and he tries to please you or make you laugh. He is interested in your whole life story. — Clint, 18

It's not possible for a guy not to like a girl he talks/spends time with on a regular basis. Guys can't have a best girl friend. — Tim, 17

He just enjoys being with you and wants to be around you. — Trevor, 14

Oh gosh, um . . . depends on the guy. Me, I will flirt and will call you everyday. I can't speak for other guys so the best way to tell might be to ask. Most of us don't like the chasing thing—it's complicated and we don't read your "hints." We like blunt, so yeah, if you don't know, just ask. — Ben, 17

If a guy is trying to flirt with you or look at you and treats you really nice, you can tell it's something more. If you don't see that, chances are that he is really shy or just wants to be friends. — Logan, 16

The way he acts around you. If he's playfully mean and always jokes around, he probably likes you. — Alex, 15

Well, if he makes an effort to be near you a lot, that's one way to tell. He might pick on you too. — Chris, 16

If he goes out of his way to be near you or talk to you. — Matt, 16

If he tries to do stuff with you away from school—if he talks to you a lot and asks questions or he gets all smiley and twinkle-eyed. — Cabe, 14

If he does things for you that he doesn't do for his other friends. — Matthew, 16

To Sum It Up:

We couldn't help but notice that MOST Christian guys:

- **are drawn to girls who put their relationship with Christ above all else.**

- *are attracted to confident girls who aren't afraid to be themselves.*

- **hate drama.**

- *don't care much for mean girls.*

- **wish girls would wear more clothes.**

- *think girls are loose and desperate for attention when they dress immodestly.*

- **say looks are important but inner beauty is a must.**

- *are wired by God to think about sex.*

- **would rather talk all day and get to know a girl than kiss her for an hour.**

- *will make an effort to be around a girl if they like her (translation: no need to chase them down).*

- **value what their friends think about a girl they may like and may decide not to pursue her if they get a bad report (translation: if you care about your reputation, keep that in mind).**

- *are not near as simple as they claim to be.* ✱

- **think a lot about sports, video games, and fireworks.**

- *don't think about girls 24/7, but they are certainly on their minds.*

weigh in @ virtuous reality .com

YOUR QUESTIONS about GUYS

answered by SUSIE DAVIS

1. **It's commonly accepted that women are more complicated and men only think about their basic needs. What do you think about this?**

Men think only about their basic needs? What exactly are "basic needs" anyway? Food and water? A place to sleep? Grunt, grunt . . . come on! Men are just like women in the fact that they are made in the likeness of God. In Genesis 1:26–27 it is recorded, "Then God said, 'Let Us make man in Our image, according to Our likeness. They will rule the fish of the sea, the birds of the sky, the animals, all the earth, and the creatures that crawl on the earth.' So God created man in His own image; He created him in the image of God; He created them male and female". Since men and women are made in God's image we are all created beautiful, unique, and complex. All of us—men and women.

I think the answer you are looking for depends on the way you define complicated. If complicated means that guys are different than girls in the ways they think about relationship issues, etc., then yes, guys are less "complicated." Typically, they don't sit around pondering the relational dynamics of the people they care most about. They don't usually analyze words or actions with the intensity that is more ordinary for girls trying to figure relationships out. Guys generally handle relationships differently than girls. That's that. But to stereotype all guys as "uncomplicated" because they don't think like girls do is just wrong. And another quick note, when a guy refers to himself as "not that complicated" or "simple" (check out the survey results on the guy panel), he is not necessarily agreeing to an overall negative stereotypical generalization. What he might be saying is he doesn't do all the drama in relationships. (I know, I know—not a fair stereotype of girls in general!)

I think the basis for the question in some ways reflects two thought patterns in society. The first is that girls in general are attracted to guys and extremely curious to understand them. I want to affirm that—it's a good thing. Now, the second thing I am concerned it might reflect is this notion that men are somewhat uncomplicated or stupid. Just watch TV to catch this mentality. The man is the buffoon who doesn't understand women, childrearing, or life in general. The trick here is that the media has pounced on a man's differences in general and exaggerated them to make him seem like a fool. Not a good thing. The truth is we, as women, need to be extremely careful to realize that while men and women have some innate differences, that is not all bad and it certainly doesn't mean all men are "uncomplicated" in this negative sense.

There is a passage in Psalm 139:1–15 (CEV) that I want to use as an example of the male thought pattern. This particular psalm was written by King David who is obviously a man and it is perhaps one of the most descriptively written passages in the Bible concerning the internal human makeup and thought pattern. In parenthesis highlighted in green, you can see my notes debunking the idea that men are nonthinking, uncomplicated losers.

You have looked deep into my heart (He acknowledges he has a heart here and one capable of depth too), LORD, and you know all about me. You know when I am resting or when I am working, and from heaven you discover my thoughts (Thoughts . . . he is having some whether hanging out or at work). You notice everything I do and

everywhere I go (He is basically acknowledging God's omniscience which in itself is a big and complicated idea). Before I even speak a word, you know what I will say, and with your powerful arm you protect me from every side (A need for protection? Yes, even guys understand they are not invincible and could use some

...: We are all created beautiful, unique, and complex. All of us— MEN & WOMEN.

The trick here is that the media has pounced on a man's differences in general and exaggerated them to make him seem like a fool.

help from above). I can't understand all of this! (Ah—ha! He gets that he doesn't get it all—this is called humility—and a really nice trait in a man.) Such wonderful knowledge is far above me. Where could I go to escape from your Spirit or from your sight? If I were to climb up to the highest heavens, you would be there. If I were to dig down to the world of the dead you would also be there. Suppose I had wings like the dawning day and flew across the ocean. Even then your powerful arm would guide and protect me. Or suppose I said, "I'll hide in the dark until night comes to cover me over." But you see in the dark because daylight and dark are all the same to you. (OK—this whole last section, aside from being every Lit teacher's dream because it's so beautifully written—is all about David acknowledging God's control over his life. You gotta love that!) You are the one who put me together inside my mother's body, and I praise you because of the wonderful way you created me. (Think about the tenderness of a man writing about being inside of his mother's womb—this guy is poetic and sensitive!) Everything you do is marvelous! Of this I have no doubt. (Giving God credit for his wonderful work—I like it.) Nothing about me is hidden from you! (Reads: I am understood by you God.)

Now, while all the guys in your life aren't likely spouting off with the kind of wisdom and eloquence of King David, they are certainly capable of doing so. And because they, as well as we, are capable of such thought and emotion and understanding, let's make sure we treat each other as such. We're all pretty complicated and unique in the most positive sense possible because we mirror a God that has created us just like him.

2. **Do you think it's advisable to pray with your boyfriend? Or should you pray separately from your boyfriend about the relationship?**

I love this question. I love it because it says to me that you are a girl who is seeking to place God first in your relationships.

Let me just start by saying that Christian opinion is all over the book on this answer. I have talked with some women who fervently feel that prayer is way too personal to involve a boyfriend in. And there are some women who think that praying together is perfectly appropriate and normal for Christian couples—even those that are dating.

The key here is the fact that everyone who has something to say about whether or not to pray with your boyfriend realizes that all the talk is just that—talk. It's opinion. There are no specific, drop-dead instructions in the Bible on whether you should or should not pray with your boyfriend. There are no verses in the Bible that support or condemn the practice. No answers on that one—no right or wrong. My best advice? Ask God. He will direct you. He sees your heart. He knows what is best for you. ✱

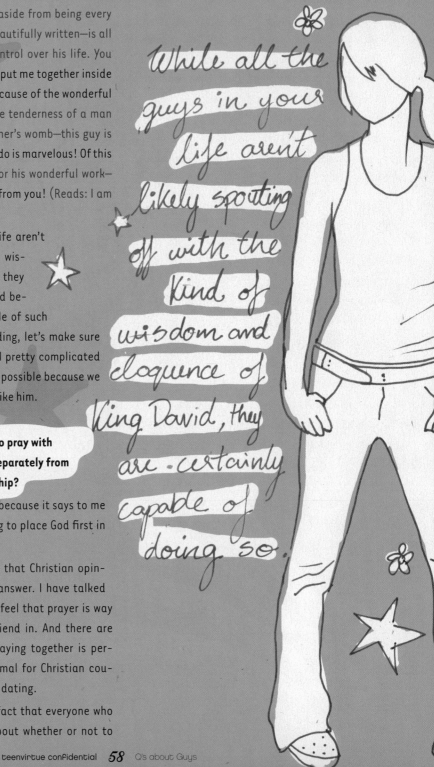

While all the guys in your life aren't likely spouting off with the kind of wisdom and eloquence of King David, they are certainly capable of doing so.

Q's ABOUT BODY DEVELOPMENT & SEX

HOW FAR IS TOO FAR?

by Vicki Courtney

Ahhh, the ever-popular "how far is too far question?" If I had to list the top three questions I get off my ministry Web site for teen girls, virtuousreality.com, or at events, this one would definitely make the cut. I personally don't think there is one hard and fast answer that is true for everyone when it comes to this question.

Depending on whom you ask, some Christians will say kissing is too far, while yet, others say it is anything beyond the kiss. The real question is at what point do you personally, hit the point of no return? For many, it is possible to draw the line at kissing and resist the temptation to want to go beyond that. Some may find it very difficult to stop at just a kiss and will need to draw the line before that. I would highly suggest some basic rules to ensure

that you don't cross the line. Don't put yourself in situations where you will be alone with your boyfriend for extended periods of time. No lying down next to each other. No snuggling under covers. Also, there's a big difference between "kissing" and "making out." A "kiss" is more like the punctuation at the end of a sentence. "Making out" is an open-ended sentence that invites a variety of different endings.

Now, I realize many of you are reading this and thinking, *C'mon, lady—do you know how hard it would* be to draw the line at a kiss? I do. And I realize that very few of you will have a 100 percent success rate in doing so. Survey results back it up: Christian or not, our bodies are wired to desire physical intimacy and to say no is a difficult challenge for many. However, in spite of what the culture implies, we are not sex-craved animals that must satisfy the urges within. Another challenge in the battle to remain pure (and one that I hear few Christians address) is the fact that the average age of marriage continues to increase over the years for both men and women. In Bible times, it was not uncommon for teens to marry very young. It is speculated that Mary, the mother of Jesus, was as young as fourteen to sixteen years old when she gave birth. Today, the average age of marriage is nearly twenty-six for women and twenty-eight for men. It makes you wonder if the same God, who gives us raging hormones in our teen years (in order that it would encourage us to marry and bear children), ever intended that we wait almost a decade longer (or more) to enjoy sex. Food for thought. I am certainly not suggesting

that this gives teens permission to go for it when it comes to sexual activity. Nor, am I suggesting that you get married in your teen years. I am, however, suggesting that we question our culture's mentality of delayed marriage into the mid-late twenties and beyond.

If you are asking the question "How far is too far?" let me give you a list of some things you might want to avoid to help you in the battle to stay pure:

- dating a guy who doesn't hold your same values and beliefs,
- dating a guy who doesn't have the same boundary line and respect your boundary line,
- being alone with your boyfriend for extended periods of time,
- watching shows and movies that depict sex and sexual activity as a recreational hobby,

- reading sexually suggestive books (romance novels and smutty teen fiction like Gossip Girls), and

- not having a firm game plan for where your boundary line is—figure it out on the front end rather than after the fact!

Here are some things you will need if you are to stand up to the challenge:

- **prayer** (on a regular basis); pour your heart out to God and keep the lines of communication open. Tell him you are struggling . . . ask him to help you remain pure.

- **accountability**: tell at least one Christian friend or mentor where your boundary line is and ask them to check in with you to see how you're doing. Also, ask them to pray for you.

- time spent in **God's Word** on a regular basis: this is where your strength will come from—without it, your tank will eventually run dry.

Regardless of when (or if) you marry, God expects you to maintain your sexual purity. It is not impossible to draw a boundary that is pleasing to God and stick with it. No, it will not be easy. Yes, some of you may slip up along the way, but this does not mean you grow callous to sexual sin and continue in that sin. It's never too late to do the right thing. ✱

weigh in @ virtuous reality .com

The following answers are taken from The Medical Institute for Sexual Health, Melissa R. Cox, editor, *Questions Kids Ask About Sex: Honest Answers for Every Age* (Grand Rapids, MI, 2005).

1. What actually happens during sex?

During the process of sexual arousal when a man "gets excited," blood vessels in the penis are filled (engorged) with blood. This causes the penis to get longer and harder and is called an erection. When the penis is erect and is inserted into the woman's vagina, it can be incredibly pleasurable. At the height or climax of these pleasurable feelings (called an orgasm), the man's body releases semen (fluid containing the sperm). This is called ejaculation. (*Questions Kids Ask About Sex*, 163)

2. What is a virgin?

A virgin is a person who has never had sexual intercourse. Many teens falsely assume that they are virgins if they've only had oral sex. This simply is not true. Oral sex can place you at tremendous risk for physical and emotional consequences. Therefore, having oral sex does indicate that a person is no longer a virgin. In addition to the standard definition of *sexual intercourse*, *Merriam-Webster's Medical Dictionary* also defines sexual intercourse as "intercourse involving genital contact between individuals other than penetration of the vagina by the penis." (*Questions Kids Ask About Sex*, 129)

3. What does promiscuous mean?

Webster's dictionary defines promiscuous as "indiscriminate." Another definition for promiscuous is having more than one sexual partner. Today, being promiscuous suggests that one has had or has multiple sexual partners. (*Questions Kids Ask About Sex,* 186)

4. What is an STD? I heard that you can get STD's from toilet seats. Is that true?

Sexually transmitted disease (STD) and sexually transmitted infection (STI) are terms now used for what used to be called venereal disease (VD). STDs are the result of an infection with various types of "germs"—gonorrhea and syphilis. Examples of viruses are HIV, genital herpes, hepatitis B, and human papillomavirus. Thrichomoniasis is caused by a trichomonas vaginalis.

Most STIs are spread almost exclusively by intimate sexual contact and usually infect the genital area, mouth, or rectum. STIs aren't spread from toilet seats, shaking hands, or other nonsexual contact. (*Questions Kids Ask About Sex,* 270)

5. A lot of my friends are "hooking up" for casual sex. What can I say to them to help them stop?

One thing teens don't think about when they are "hooking up" is that they are not just having sex with that individual but with all of his previous partners and his partners' partners. Most people who are willing to hook-up have probably had multiple sex partners, so the odds of getting an STI or STD are high. Try telling your friends that one! (*Questions Kids Ask About Sex,* 257)

6. Is it true that pretty much everyone is doing it?

This is simply not true. More than 50 percent of high school girls (grades nine through twelve) have never had sex. Repeated surveys show that teens think more of their peers are sexually active than actually are. Surveys also show that the majority of sexually experienced high school students wish they had waited longer to have sex. (*Questions Kids Ask About Sex,* 188)

7. What is "secondary virginity"?

Secondary virginity is a term for a person who has been sexually active in the past but makes the decision to not have sex again until marriage. Anyone, at any time, can decide to stop having sex and wait for marriage.

(*Questions Kids Ask About Sex*, 232)

8. Sometimes I have feelings for girls. Does this mean I'm gay?

Homosexual feelings and curiosities are normal, passing feelings that many teenagers this age experience. Almost all teenagers have had a concern about homosexual tendencies. Homosexual curiosity doesn't mean you're homosexual. Feelings and attraction aren't always under one's control. Behavior choices are controllable. Choosing to engage in homosexual behavior can be physically and emotionally dangerous. I would encourage you to talk to a trusted adult who can help you think and talk through the many feelings and emotions you may have. (*Questions Kids Ask About Sex*, 201) ✳

TOUGH QUESTIONS

1. IS IT NORMAL TO WONDER WHAT IT'S LIKE TO KISS A GUY?

(answered by Vicki Courtney)

Absolutely! In fact, I remember a sleepover in my middle school years where we joked around and practiced kissing on our pillows. (I know, I know . . . promise me you'll never share this story!) There was one girl in the bunch who had kissed a boy or two, so she gave us step-by-step instructions on how to give the perfect movie star kiss. My, my, what a difference a couple of years can make. In elementary school we were all screaming "Gross!" when we saw a kiss like that on a movie screen and now here we were making out with our pillows!

It is normal to feel all sorts of apprehension about kissing. *What if you are a bad kisser? What if he tells all his friends? What if word gets around and you never get kissed again?* Who knew that kissing could be so stressful? All the more

reason to make sure you save that first kiss (or next kiss) for someone very special. A romantic kiss is a form of affection that says, "I'm really into you." God never intended for kisses to be swapped casually in a game of Truth or Dare, a dark movie theater, or a casual, meaningless hook-up. There will be plenty of girls who are willing to kiss plenty of boys just to experience that momentary thrill of the moment . . .

over and over again. And I won't lie to you—kissing can be pretty thrilling! Girls who kiss for sport will quickly find that the initial thrill eventually wears off. These are usually the same girls who are willing to give out more than just a kiss in search of the next biggest thrill and, in the process, compromise their sexual purity. I know it sounds impossible, but wait until the moment is right. I have taught my boys that they should never kiss a girl unless they are in a serious dating relationship. I tell them often, "If she's not special enough to date, she's not yours to kiss." And then I throw a pillow at them. ☺ Trust me, a kiss saved for that special person is worth the wait.

2. IF YOU ARE DATING A GUY WHO HAS DIFFERENT VIEWS ABOUT SEX BEFORE MARRIAGE THAN YOU DO, SHOULD THAT BE A DEAL BREAKER?

(answered by Sarah Cameron and Kristin Cameron)

Sex is a sacred gift that God created exclusively for married couples to experience and enjoy. God does not call us to abstain from sex before marriage as a form of punishment or to test our strength and obedience to him, but he calls us to abstain because he loves us. God created sex as an expression of intimacy and love that is supposed to closely bind a husband and wife. In the book of Hebrews, God clearly expresses his intention for sex to be confined to marriage: "Marriage should be honored by all, and the marriage bed kept pure, for God will judge the adulterer and all the sexually immoral" (13:4 NIV).

As girls we desire to be romanced and pursued by that special guy and sadly, many girls will do whatever it takes to keep the attention coming, including giving up one of their most sacred gifts from God, their virginity. I have seen friends make the mistake of giving away their precious virginity to boys they

a) not a Christian, or b) a Christian who is living for himself rather than for God. The Bible commands that we not be unequally yoked in our relationships (see 2 Corinthians 6:14). No guy is worth compromising your beliefs . . . ever.

"madly in love with" at the time. They rationalize it, convinced that it must "be right" if it "feels right." Eventually, the break-up occurs and they are left with the guilt and heartache that follows. Some will choose to numb the pain by remaining sexually active and giving in to just about any guy who

3. IS IT WEIRD TO BE REALLY EXCITED ABOUT GETTING TO HAVE SEX ONCE I'M MARRIED? (answered by Vicki Courtney)

No, not at all! In fact, if you weren't somewhat excited, I would be concerned. Sometimes Christian teens hear the "don't do it until you're married" message so often that some may walk away with the misunderstanding that sex is not a good thing. It is even possible that some Christian teens (more

shows the slightest interest in them.

Moral of the story? If a guy thinks that sex before marriage is OK and encourages you to think the same way, then you should run as fast as you can in the other direction! When dating, it's very important that you consider the character of the guy you are going out with. If he's pressuring you to have sex, he is either:

likely, the girls) may carry a negative image of sex into marriage. It's important that teens understand God's view of sex and develop an appropriate balance in their thinking. Sex outside of marriage can produce negative consequences, which can be a bad thing. But that does not mean sex itself is bad. In the context of marriage, sex is a wonderful thing! God wired our bodies to want to have sex in order that we would procreate and popu-

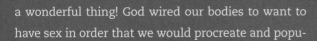

late the earth. He also created sex to be an act of love between a husband and a wife. In addition to it being physically pleasurable, it creates an emotional bond, as well. Ephesians 5:31 says, "For this reason a man will leave his father and mother and be united to his wife, and the two will become one flesh." It was never God's intent that we become "one flesh" with someone other than our spouse. God says to wait and therefore, we must wait. His boundary is in place to protect us from the physical, emotional, and spiritual consequences that can occur when sex is practiced outside of marriage. In the meantime, it is perfectly normal to think about it from time to time and look forward to experiencing sex in marriage.

4. IS IT NORMAL TO DAYDREAM ABOUT SEXUAL FANTASIES?

(answered by Vicki Courtney)

It is normal to have thoughts about sex and wonder what it is like. Where it gets dangerous is when we welcome those thoughts and build upon them. Just because an inappropriate thought pops into your head, it doesn't make it a sin. Choosing to entertain the thought does. For example, maybe you have a crush on a guy at your school who gives you attention from time to time. You imagine what it would be like to be alone with him and even kiss him. Before long, you have built an entire script around that one thought. You create the circumstances, the loca-

tion, the tender words of affection, and the happy ending—the lip lock. But the next time you retreat into fantasy la-la land, it goes beyond the kiss. So, what's the harm, you ask? In the book, *Every Young Woman's Battle*, the author makes the excellent point that "thinking equals

rehearsing." She says that "when you fantasize about sexually or emotionally inappropriate behavior with someone, you are basically rehearsing a scenario of

what you would say and do if you were alone with that person. Rehearsing can set you up to act it out if the opportunity were to present itself."

Every Young Woman's Battle also suggests that you can "train your mind to mind." It says that "you can't keep from being tempted, but you can avoid rehearsing and you can certainly refuse to act on a tempting thought. You can train your mind to mind. No temptation becomes sin without your permission." So, how do you stop the thoughts from sprouting into a full-blown fantasy? The book suggests "bouncing your thoughts." What this means is to "rehearse" in your mind doing or saying the right thing. Bounce the inappropriate thought with an appropriate one.

Finally, Philippians 4:8 says, "Fix your thoughts on what is true and honorable and right. Think about things that are pure and lovely and admirable. Think about things that are excellent and worthy of praise" (NLT). We should always be able to think of things that are worthy of praise. When inappropriate thoughts pop into your head, turn them off and turn on the praise. Before long, you will cultivate a healthy habit of praise rather than allowing sin to take its course.

5. IS MASTURBATION WRONG?

(answered by Vicki Courtney)

One of the best answers I have read on the subject of masturbation is from the book *Every Young Woman's Battle* by Shannon Etheridge and Stephen Arterburn. They say, "If you feel tempted to masturbate, it doesn't mean that you are a bad person, only that you are a human being with sexual desires and passions, as all of us are." I couldn't agree with them more.

So, is it wrong? Below are some reasons listed in *Every Young Woman's Battle* as to why masturbation is unhealthy:

- Masturbation can be habit-forming and addictive.

- Masturbation does not satisfy sexual desires, it intensifies them. If you give in to your sexual desires through masturbation, you do not gain practice in exercising self-control. What hope will you have when some smooth-talking guy starts whispering sweet nothings into your ear if you can't even control your desires when alone?

- Habitual sin can cause us to feel distanced from God and from the ones we love.

- Masturbation is not healthy because it can train a person to "fly solo," to operate independently of anyone else. When you marry, if your husband isn't able to please you in the exact same way, this could make your marital sex life very frustrating and disappointing.

Shannon Etheridge and Stephen Arterburn, *Every Young Woman's Battle* (Colorado Springs, CO: Waterbrook Press, 2004).

Most importantly, the book points out "once you awaken your sexual desires, which masturbation does, you will find them very difficult to put back to sleep."

I realize that the world treats masturbation like it's no big deal, but in truth, you are making a trade. Anything that causes you to feel distant from God should be avoided. *

the 411 on Your Period

by Susie Davis

Need some information on what's going on with your body but too embarrassed to ask? That's pretty normal for girls your age. As a matter of fact, many grown women are weirded out about asking questions too. Honestly, unless you're a doctor or on your way to med school, talking about body function—and especially body function from "those parts"—makes most people a little uncomfortable. So here's the deal. I am going to unpack some of the mystery and you read away; just make sure that no one is peering over your shoulder so you don't have to answer any awkward questions. The questions are bolded and the answers follow to find out all about the 411 on periods.

. . . . It is typical to wonder if you are "normal" physically . . . .

regarding their development. But what I do want you to know is that it is typical to wonder if you are "normal" physically—especially if you are comparing yourself to the girls around you. It can be difficult to have all your friends start their period when you haven't. On one hand, you are likely relieved that you don't have to bother with the things your friends are experiencing, and on the other hand, you probably have some nagging doubts about whether you will ever even get your period.

Most of my friends have started theirs and I haven't. Am I normal?

This one is somewhat difficult to answer because I don't know anything about where you are in your physical development and I'm not a doctor. I can tell you that girls start their periods anywhere between the ages of eight and seventeen. And the girls who start on the very early or very late side are best to speak with their doctors

Why is it called a period?

The medical name for a period is called the menstrual cycle, menses, or menstrual period. None of those really roll off the tongue, so women everywhere have come up with lots of different nicknames for the menstrual cycle and "period" is just a shortened version of the above. It is by far the most popular and most often used.

What all happens during a period?

The process of the menstrual cycle is really amazing. It all starts in the hypothalamus, which is located at the base of the brain. The hypothalamus is relatively small for the enormous job it does in your body. It is responsible for signaling the start of puberty by giving your pituitary gland a kick start. Once the pituitary glands get going on this mission, they send a message to your ovaries. You have two ovaries and they are responsible for releasing an egg (which you absolutely cannot see without a microscope) and secreting two hormones: estrogen and progesterone. This egg is released monthly through your fallopian tubes (the ovaries generally take turns releasing an egg) and if the egg is unfertilized, then the egg and the outermost lining of the uterus, the endometrial tissue, dies and sloughs off resulting in a period. Most periods last five to seven days.

A regular schedule is roughly every twenty-eight days.

gynecologist (a doctor that specializes in physical care of the reproductive system of women).

Does it hurt to have a period?

It doesn't hurt to have your period. The sloughing process is not painful in itself; however, cramping can occur as well as some bloating, which can cause discomfort. Taking Advil or Tylenol relieves many symptoms. If you are having excruciating pain, tell your mom and consider the possibility of seeing a gynecologist.

I have heard that tampons hurt— is that true?

While tampon use should not hurt, learning to insert and remove one can cause some discomfort. Make sure and look into getting a tampon that will work for you. If you are new to using tampons, search for the smaller, slender ones. Make sure after you insert the tampon that you wrap up the applicator in toilet tissue and throw it in the trash. No one wants to see those used applicators —yuck! Also, inside every package of tampons there should be instructions and warnings. Be sure to read about toxic shock syndrome and take steps to avoid it by alternating tampons and pads. Especially consider using pads at night so you don't accidentally leave your tampons in too long. (Too long is more than 4 to 6 hours.)

What if I start my period and then it stops?

Irregular periods are normal the first year you start. Irregularity is sometimes seen when you skip a month or several months or if you have a very light period with hardly any bleeding. But after a year from the start of your first period, your periods should settle into a more regular schedule. A regular schedule is roughly every twenty-eight days. If after a year, your periods are still irregular (more than one a month or skipping many months between periods) or extremely heavy (meaning you are bleeding more that eight days or experiencing heavy soaking of more than eight pads or tampons per day), then you need to see a doctor. Tell your mom or a trusted woman friend and make an appointment with a

I'm worried people will know when I'm on my period. Will they?

No one can tell when you are on your period. But remember to keep track on a calendar when you have your period so that you can be aware of when to expect it. It can be very embarrassing to leak through your clothes in public because you weren't expecting it. If you want to be extra careful, always carry a pad or tampon in your purse or backpack just in case.

My friends complain that their period makes their face break out—does it?

Sometimes a pimple or two might show up right before or during your period. It has to do with the hormones surging to get your body ready to do its reproductive job. While pimples can be embarrassing, remember there are very few people who go through teenage years without getting some blemishes. Wash your face daily with soap and water; and if you are really having trouble with acne-like skin issues, try to get in and see a dermatologist who can provide medicines especially for your skin type and condition.

Well, there you go—some 411 on your period.

And if you need more info, ask your mom. It's a good idea to understand your body, even the parts that are kind of complicated. And honestly, there's no reason to be embarrassed because the way your body works is miraculous. And it is wonderfully made by God. Though you might feel like your period is a curse at times, it is actually one of the biggest blessings of being a woman. The fact that your body is functioning in this way means that you are likely able to have a baby—at the right time (when you're married) with the right man (your husband) and that can be absolutely amazing. ✳

Though you might feel like your period is a curse at times, it is actually one of the biggest blessings of being a woman.

The Medical Institute for Sexual Health, Melissa R. Cox, editor, *Questions Kids Ask About Sex: Honest Answers for Every Age* (Grand Rapids, MI, 2005), 151.

YOUR QUESTIONS ABOUT BODY DEVELOPMENT

1. WHY DO WE HAVE BOOBS? ARE MINE TOO SMALL?
(answered by Susie Davis)

Boobs—that's kind of a weird word and the correct term is actually breasts, but who in the world goes around calling them that? If you look up *boob* in the dictionary it says: a stupid awkward person. Not at all what we think of when we hear the word *boob*. There are always tons of nicknames for gender specific body parts. I guess because people get so embarrassed discussing "private parts." Why, for breasts alone I bet you can think of some nicknames you've heard in the halls at school. Like maybe tits, lady lumps, melons, jugs, rack, and my all time favorite slang term for breasts: The Girls. Yes, Stacey and Clinton on "What Not to Wear" delicately refer to breasts as "The Girls." (At least they created a gender specific slang term for that womanly body part.)

So first, let's tackle the "why boobs" question. Three answers here. First, your breasts distinguish your body as uniquely female. Those shapely curves sitting on your chest create a body that says quite clearly, "I'm a woman." Now, right now that might be the last thing you want your body to say, and you'd rather just stuff your "girls" in a sports bra to silence them—some day you might think differently.

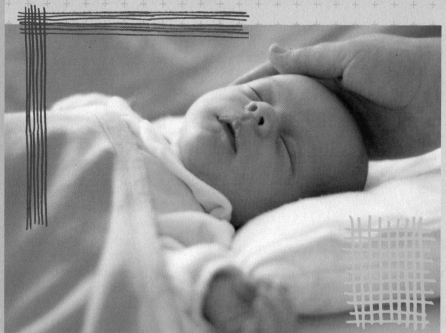

delight! You are tall and slim like a palm tree, and your breasts are like its clusters of dates. I said, 'I will climb up into the palm tree and take hold of its branches.' Now may your breasts be like grape clusters, and the scent of your breath like apples. May your kisses be as exciting as the best wine, smooth and sweet, flowing gently over lips and teeth" (NLT). As you can read, this man is all about the woman's body bringing him pleasure, in particular, her "clusters." So boobs are about enjoyable sex (for the man and the woman). And obviously God is all about encouraging it in marriage or he wouldn't have it in the Bible.

Now, how about the size issue? Are your boobs too small? Too small for what? Breast feeding? No, I don't think that is what you were asking. So the only other thing I can figure is you were asking if they are too small to be appealing to a man. Do me a favor, reread the verse above. It's kind of interesting to note

Second, your breasts are there to feed your future children. The fact is your body, upon pregnancy, will have the capability to feed your child. That is completely amazing. (And aside from that, think of the convenience.) Also note this: breast milk is the perfect food for an infant. It has all the nutrients that an infant needs most in the appropriate amounts. In addition, it contains antibodies that protect an infant from illness. It comes in at the perfect temperature in the most sterile environment possible. And all this because new mothers have breasts filled with milk for their babies.

Third answer to the "why boobs" question: enjoyable sex. Breasts are often referred to as a sex organ because they are capable of sexual stimulation. There is even a book in the Bible that mentions this phenomenon. It's called the Song of Solomon and within the book there are all kinds of references to sexual love. Read these verses in Song of Solomon 7:6–9, "Oh, how delightful you are, my beloved; how pleasant for utter

that Solomon compares his lover's breasts to date and grape clusters. Ever seen a date . . . how about a grape? Little. The point here is that men like all kinds of breasts. Big or little. They like the fact that women have them. And the real issue with your question is that you are likely wondering if your breasts are attractive to guys. Let me say simply that they are (or will be if you are still developing), and you need to remember: there is no right or wrong size. Size is relative to your physical frame and attractiveness is all about preference. While media and culture may be communicating big breasts as the most beautiful breasts right now, realize that culture changes its mind about beauty and size as often as the weather. The best thing you can do is thank God he gave you such an amazing, versatile body with all it's properly formed and functioning parts. And beautiful at that.

2. I CAN NEVER BE PERFECT LIKE THE GIRLS IN MAGAZINES, ON TELEVISION, OR IN THE MOVIES. WHY WOULD ANYBODY WANT ME THE WAY I AM?

(answered by Sarah Cameron)

I remember asking myself that same exact question at your age. It was usually after flipping through a fashion magazine and seeing the seemingly perfect models with sparkling white teeth, slender legs, flawless skin, and the cutest outfits imaginable. And here I was—short with stubby muscular legs, less-than-perfect skin, rather boring hair, and to top it all off, a set of shiny braces. I looked nothing like the gorgeous girls in the magazine, and the more I thought about it, the more my physical appearance depressed me. I wanted to be a popular girl, surrounded by people who loved me and wanted to be my friend. I thought that the only way to be loved and accepted in this way was to be physically attractive.

That same year, I tried out for my school's dance team, a group of girls known for being popular and beautiful. After making the team, I thought I had it made. Working hard everyday in practice, I soon

became one of the better dancers, which caused the others to pay more attention to me. In the locker room everyday, the girls would be really friendly and help me straighten my hair, fix my eye shadow, or give me a spray of their designer perfume. Soon I knew how to walk and talk like a popular pretty girl, and I took pride in my position on the team. There

was nothing better than strutting through the halls on the day of a pep rally decked out in my uniform. I thought I was one of the coolest girls in the school.

However, the happiness I felt was short-lived. Later in my sophomore year, I realized that most of the girls had nothing more than skin-deep beauty. They knew how to apply mascara really well and had fashion-

able wardrobes, but most of them were empty on the inside. Though I was a Christian, most of the girls weren't believers, a fact that became more apparent as I saw their behavior. Every morning I was surrounded by girls that did a number of things I knew didn't make God happy including drinking, smoking, cussing, and gossiping. And even though they appeared to have it all, before long I began to realize how consumed they were with the outside rather than the inside. Over a year's time, my desire to fit in with these girls had hurt my relationship with God. I eventually ended up quitting the team and working on redefining my definition of "beauty." As I developed friendships with other people, I focused more on their internal beauty than their outward appearance. In doing so, I found genuine friends that loved me for the beautiful person I am on the inside.

Most importantly, I worked on my walk with the Lord and asked him to help me develop qualities the Spirit commands all Christians to have, those of "love, joy, peace, patience, kindness, goodness, faithfulness, gentleness, and self-control" (Galatians 5:22–23 NIV). Next time you see girls who look "perfect" on the outside, remember that many are empty on the inside. True beauty will begin in the heart. Proverbs 31:30 says, "Charm is deceptive and beauty is fleeting, but a woman who fears the Lord will be praised." To fear the Lord is to love him with

> # CHARM IS DECEPTIVE AND BEAUTY IS FLEETING, BUT A WOMAN WHO FEARS THE LORD WILL BE PRAISED.
> ## PROVERBS 31:30

all your heart, soul, mind, and strength. Oh, and by the way, when you see the models on the pages of the fashion magazines, remember that word, "fleeting." Come twenty-plus years from now, they will be past their prime. If they've put all their eggs in the outer beauty basket, their self-worth will plummet and they will be left with an empty hole in their hearts. Go for the brand of beauty that will stand the test of time. Strive to be a woman who "fears the Lord." Not even an extreme makeover can hold a candle to that.

face—they will always have to wonder if a guy likes them for who they are on the inside or for their bra size. While it may seem like most guys are drawn to the girls who are more developed, a godly, Christian guy will be drawn to the inner beauty of a girl.*

3. WHY DO GUYS SEEM TO ALWAYS GO FOR THE GIRLS WHO ARE MORE DEVELOPED?

(answered by Sarah Cameron)

I wondered the same thing when I stopped growing at 5'1" and all my friends kept sprouting (everywhere!). It must be nice to be able to buy a pair of jeans that fit without alterations . . . every single pair of my pants has been re-hemmed for my short legs. For a while, my height and other imperfections made me feel very insecure and I wondered how a guy could ever be attracted to me. However, I have since realized that the parts of me I view as imperfect, God sees as absolutely perfect, because I am "fearfully and wonderfully made" (Psalm 139:14). God doesn't make mistakes!

While it is true that some guys will only go for the more developed girls, I can tell you from experience that these guys are shallow, and they are not the kind of guys you want to be interested in. In fact, think about the dilemma the more developed girls

Did You Know?

Breast buds usually develop between the ages of seven and thirteen. Breasts can be tender in the first few months, but that feeling usually goes away.

It is not unusual for one breast to be larger than the other when breast buds develop. They usually even out as the breasts continue to develop.

Most girls do not have regular menstrual cycles until one to two years after they start.

Most girls will have their growth spurt the year before they start their period.

A girl will usually reach final adult height about two years after starting her period, but most of her growth will coincide with the start of her period.

The average adult woman is 5'4" tall, weighs 145 lbs. with a dress size of 11 to 14.

Breast tissue can continue to increase for up to three years after a girl starts her period.

The average bra size for a woman is 34B.

Sixty-four percent of women are pear-shaped when it comes to their body frame as opposed to hour-glass.

Only 6 percent of the population of women has an hourglass figure.

The fashion industry continues to make clothes to best fit the hourglass figure.

Almost one third (30.4 percent) of girls ages twelve to nineteen are overweight, and among that group, half are obese.

Fifty percent of overweight children/teens remain overweight as adults.

Children with one obese parent are twice as likely to become obese as adults.

Girls without siblings are at greater risk for becoming overweight.

Girls with older mothers are at increased risk of being overweight. ✱

Q's
**ABOUT FAITH

A WORD ABOUT FAITH
BY: GOD

Matthew 17:20 "Because of your little faith," He told them. "For I assure you: If you have faith the size of a mustard seed, you will tell this mountain, 'Move from here to there,' and it will move. Nothing will be impossible for you."

Romans 10:17 So faith comes from what is heard, and what is heard comes through the message about Christ.

1 Corinthians 16:13 Be alert, stand firm in the faith, be brave and strong.

2 Corinthians 5:7 For we walk by faith, not by sight.

2 Corinthians 13:5 Test yourselves to see if you are in the faith. Examine yourselves. Or do you not recognize for yourselves that Jesus Christ is in you?—unless you fail the test.

For by grace you are saved through faith, and this is not from yourselves; it is God's gift—not from works, so that no one can boast.
Ephesians 2:8–9

Galatians 2:19–20 For through the law I have died to the law, that I might live to God. I have been crucified with Christ; and I no longer live, but Christ lives in me. The life I now live in the flesh, I live by faith in the Son of God, who loved me and gave Himself for me.

1 Timothy 4:1 Now the Spirit explicitly says that in the latter times some will depart from the faith, paying attention to deceitful spirits and the teachings of demons.

2 Timothy 2:22 Flee from youthful passions, and pursue righteousness, faith, love, and peace, along with those who call on the Lord from a pure heart.

2 Timothy 4:7 I have fought the good fight, I have finished the race, I have kept the faith.

Hebrews 11:3 By faith we understand that the universe was created by the word of God, so that what is seen has been made from things that are not visible.

Hebrews 12:1–2 Therefore since we also have such a large cloud of witnesses surrounding us, let us lay aside every weight and the sin that so easily ensnares us, and run with endurance the race that lies before us, keeping our eyes on Jesus, the source and perfecter of our faith, who for the joy that lay before Him endured a cross and despised the shame, and has sat down at the right hand of God's throne.

Now without faith it is impossible to please God, for the one who draws near to Him must believe that He exists and rewards those who seek Him.

Hebrews 11:6

James 1:2–3 Consider it a great joy, my brothers, whenever you experience various trials, knowing that the testing of your faith produces endurance.

James 2:26 For just as the body without the spirit is dead, so also faith without works is dead.

1 John 5:3–4 For this is what love for God is: to keep His commands. Now His commands are not a burden, because whatever has been born of God conquers the world. This is the victory that has conquered the world: our faith. *

Now faith is the reality of what is hoped for, the proof of what is not seen.

Hebrews 11:1

A Leap of Faith

by Susie Davis

A couple of weeks ago, my family and I visited Camp Timberline in Estes Park, Colorado, where our son, Will, just completed his summer term as a counselor. Besides being a counselor to the kids, he also managed the ropes course. I don't know how much you know about ropes courses, but, from a novice's viewpoint, let me tell you that they look a lot like something Tarzan might have left in the jungle after a long day of playing with the monkeys. There are all kinds of ropes stretched from one tree to another high in the air. Apparently the campers like to come and climb up into the trees, attach themselves to one of the ropes, and swing out over the open ground zipping along like a flying squirrel. As I craned my neck to look up at all the lines, I decided that I very much liked my feet squarely planted on the ground and was secretly pleased that the high ropes portion of the course was closed for the time being.

One of the elements of the high ropes course was called "The Leap of Faith." In this element Will described how a camper climbs a pole (much like a telephone pole but more wobbly) and stands at the top of it (toes hanging off because it's only about twelve inches wide). The goal of the element is to jump off the pole and try to reach a trapeze bar, like at the circus but with no net underneath, which is hanging in the air some feet in front of them. The great news is that the campers get to wear two harnesses. One harness fits around their legs and waist and another harness attaches to their chest and shoulders. These harnesses are attached with a rope to a steel cable above them just in case they miss the swing. Because of this my son explained that there really should be no fear of a kid smashing into the ground below with the harness safely attached. (Thank goodness!) And yet, Will went on to say that most of the campers cautiously climb the pole, then timidly stand on the top of it, and look down the height of the pole nervously—much afraid. When they are able to think about the next move, which is to jump out from the safety of the skinny pole to catch the swing, there is more waiting as they look for other avenues of escape. The only problem is there is a rule for the campers: once you're atop the pole, the only way down is to jump out to the swing. Yikes!

Now apparently, not many campers race up the pole and throw themselves into the air toward the swing without some thought about the possible results. Not too many fail to consider the possibility of smashing their face in the soil some thirty feet below. (Sounds fun, huh?) Will told us the scariest part for the campers is that they must trust the rope attached to their back via the harness because they can't see the rope (they really need to watch where they are going instead of staring at the rope over their shoulder) and they

My form of free falling is about my belief in God and my relationship with him— it's about being a Christian.

can't feel the rope (unless of course they fall and feel the tension of it catching them). I have to confess I didn't even want to try and give "The Leap of Faith" a shot. I also had difficulty imagining hundreds of campers waiting in line to scamper up the wobbly pole for a chance to throw their bodies in the air toward the tiny swing. But quite a few gave it a try—adventurous little things—they must really like the feeling of free falling.

While I haven't put the high ropes course on my list of things to do, I actually do exercise a form of free falling pretty often. No, not in the fun and games department of my life but instead in the spiritual part of my life. And it might as well be called "The Leap of Faith" because quite often I don't see what will catch me and I sometimes feel the odds are great that I might miss the tiny swing on the other side. My form of free falling is about my belief in God and my relationship with him—it's about being a Christian.

Being a Christian is about faith. The Bible actually says that without faith, it is impossible to please God. Hebrews 11:6 says, "It's impossible to please God apart from faith. And why? Because anyone who wants to approach God must believe both that he exists and that he cares enough to respond to those who seek him" *(The Message)*. And faith itself is leaping out without seeing exactly what it is that will catch you. Hebrews 11:1 defines it like this: "Now faith is being sure of what we hope for and certain of what we do not see" (NIV).

In a small way, it is just what the kids exercised when they were on the high ropes. They could say they trusted the harnessed rope to catch them if they fell but until they were really ready to jump out there toward the swing . . . they weren't exercising belief that the rope would catch them at all. As long as they stood, scared and wondering on top of the pole, they weren't willing to risk believing the harnessed rope would do its job. And it is the same with our faith in God. While we can sit and talk about faith and talk about Jesus and talk about God—until we make a decision to accept belief in who he says he is in the Bible—we aren't exercising faith. We're just standing on the pole of life, talking about the possibilities of the rope being there to catch us. But when we go

condemn its people. He sent him to save them! No one who has faith in God's Son will be condemned" (CEV).

If you are ready to jump out and pray to become a Christian, just know that you might feel like you are free falling on the inside. But the truth is, God is way more able than a harnessed high rope. He will be there for you. Think about saying these words to God:

"God, I believe in you. I believe in Jesus Christ and I understand what the Bible says about needing to have faith. I want to have faith that you are who you say you are and that you are really there for me. I want to be in a real relationship with you. I want you to be in my life and help me. Please catch me as I jump out to you and try out this faith exercise for the first time. I'm free falling into you. Thank you for catching me."

The truth is, God is way more able than a harnessed high rope. He will be there for you.

ahead, as scary as it might seem, and jump out to God in a relationship through Jesus Christ that is when we will begin to feel the tight safe grip of God on our life.

When we pray to Jesus, though we have never seen him, and accept that he is God's Son sent to die for us, that is when we are able to have real faith. And that is the one action God is most interested in if you are standing on the pole so to speak. John 3:16–18 explains it like this: "God loved the people of this world so much that he gave his only Son, so that everyone who has faith in him will have eternal life and never really die. God did not send his Son into the world to

Romans 10:10 promises, "For it is by believing in your heart that you are made right with God, and it is by confessing with your mouth that you are saved" (NLT).

Way to go on your leap of faith to God and welcome to a whole new adventure in your life through Jesus Christ! *

*Note: If you still have questions about what it means to be a Christian, be sure to read "The Scoop on . . . Heaven" on page 92.

the small
answer
to the **big**
question:

WHY DO BAD THINGS HAPPEN?

by Susie Davis

Something happened to me in junior high that changed my life forever. It wasn't meeting Mr. Wonderful. It wasn't discovering a talent for writing that would lead me to become an author. No, it wasn't anything like that at all. Instead what happened to me led to years of asking a very difficult question over and over again: Why do bad things happen? It is a question that I have begged God to answer. And honestly, in some ways I still struggle in understanding it.

A little history: When I was fourteen, I witnessed a murder. One of my classmates walked in with a rifle and shot and killed our teacher in front of our class. I am sure you can imagine how horrific that would be. There I was sitting in class, cutting up with my friends and laughing with the teacher, and then out of nowhere this guy walked in and shot my teacher. It was extremely frightening. And it was a critical point in my life because the event created a load of excruciating doubt about God's goodness and his love. I was a Christian at the time so I knew enough to know that God was in control and that nothing ever happened without his permission. So I also knew that he allowed it to happen. He allowed a man's death. A violent, gruesome one at that. He allowed

a wife to become a widow and a child to become fatherless (my teacher had a wife and toddler at the time of his death). He also allowed me to be in the room at the time, witnessing a brutal crime. All of this wreaked havoc in my teenage brain. It created doubt about God and it created a need to understand the very hard question: Why do bad things happen? In my struggle to understand, I sought the Bible and here are some of the hard but real answers to the question.

First, the whole why *are* there bad things? Romans 5:12 puts it this way, *"Adam sinned, and that sin brought death into the world"* (CEV). Also verse 15 of Romans 5 says, *"That one sin brought death to many others"* (CEV). While that is pretty simplistic, it truly is the biblical answer to the question. Sin leaked into the world with Adam. (Before you get too mad at Adam, read Genesis 3 to find out who else was involved in the first act of sin.) When the sin leaked in, it was as if a horrible cauldron of unspeakable ugliness and hurt spilled out too. And the spill landed all over every single person from the beginning of time until the end of all time. This one word, *death,* equals all the awful things we question and ponder including the actual act of dying. It equals 9/11, tsunamis, earthquakes, hurricanes, murder, etc., and any other thing that creates unbearable heartache in life. It equals divorce, abandonment, and hate. It equals conceit and bigotry. It equals all things that are not God. The death that entered the world when Adam sinned is the very thing that separates us from God. And while we would all like to blame Adam for all the heartache, the Bible clearly states that we all fall short of God's standard and make sin choices. Romans 3:23 puts it this way, *"For all have sinned; all fall short of God's glorious standard"* (NLT). Those sin choices create chaos in life. They did in Adam's life and they do in ours too. So the whole sin condition equals up to the fact that no one is exempt from the chaos of sin, either the participation in sin or the resulting consequence of sin. When Adam entered the world and made the wrong choice, the cauldron was opened and we all got infected with the sin disease. And this sin disease is the thing that creates heartache situations.

The nasty problem with sin of course is not only how your sin affects you but how it will also affect other people. For example, in my situation the student's sinful choice to shoot my teacher impacted the teacher's wife, son, family, friends, and all the students in the class. We all felt the blow of that sin. The difficulty of sin is realizing that as much as we are tempted to point a finger and blame others for all the hurt in the world, we are responsible for creating hurt too. In this way, we all become accomplices to the whole question of pain and suffering. If I am tempted to point my finger at my classmate and blame him, I must biblically accept that I am responsible for paining people in my life also. And then if I want to point the finger at God and ask, "Why all the pain?!" I then must biblically accept that God's best plan was not for

No one is exempt from the chaos of sin, either the participation in sin or the resulting consequence of sin.

There is always a chance for more sin and more pain and more unspeakable sadness. It can seem fairly hopeless.

all of us to act this way when he gave us freedom of choice by creating so much pain and suffering for each other. So then, if I am able to swallow all that spiritual reasoning, I often come up feeling beaten up and defeated, realizing there is always a chance for more sin and more pain and more unspeakable sadness. It can seem fairly hopeless.

But God didn't create us for hopelessness in life and there is another set of verses in Romans that help us understand God's plan for the problem of sin. It follows the whole Adam predicament and goes like this, *"Yet in an even greater way, Jesus Christ alone brought God's gift of kindness to many people. There is a lot of difference between Adam's sin and God's gift. That one sin led to punishment. But God's gift made it possible for us to be acceptable to him, even though*

we have sinned many times" (Romans 5:15–16 CEV). Also in Romans 5:20 it says, *"Yet where sin was powerful, God's kindness was even more powerful"* (CEV). The final biblical perspective to the problem? God's kindness is the most powerful piece. When he sent Jesus to deal with the sin and pain problem, his love and kindness became King. Desperation is often created when there is no hope. But God did not leave us without hope or without a comfort in horrible times. Instead, he provided Jesus as the final say on any doubts about God's goodness and his love.

OK, now that I have biblically answered the question, I have a confession to make. When I was trying to get over why my teacher was murdered, knowing the biblical answer to the question did not help me feel a lot better about my situation. Instead I spent years sorting out the pain I was feeling. I spent years dealing with the consequences of seeing something that violent. I had tons of fear issues that resulted in anxiety seeping into my life. Anxiety about God's goodness and love. About his provision for my life as an individual. I grappled with the question: *Did God step out of the room just when I needed him most?* I had trouble trusting that he really was able to take care of me and make good decisions for my life. I didn't know if I could trust him, really trust him, with all of my life. That disconnect from his trust resulted in lots of soul searching. The pain in my life pushed me out to a place where I was alone in the world trying very hard to protect myself. There was a cauldron of pain that spilled out and it took years of emotional and spiritual reckoning to deal with all the consequences I felt in my life. I didn't so much want to know *why it happened* as much as I needed to know *how to deal with what happened.* It took years of God carefully and tenderly unfolding comfort in my life. It took years to gain hope in God's plan and his goodness over my life. I am telling you this because many times when people feel the effects of tragedy firsthand, knowing the "sin entered the world through Adam" answer is the farthest thing from what they need. Instead, they need time and lots of mercy. They need prayer. And sometimes they need a friend who will grieve with them. At the end of all reasoning, they need God in the most real way possible. God wiping away their tears and planting new hope in their life, just like he did for me. ✶

God did not leave us without hope or without a comfort in horrible times. He provided Jesus . . .

THE SCOOP ON

WHAT it TAKES TO GO TO

by Vicki Courtney

AT SOME POINT IN MOST EVERYONE'S LIFE, THEY WONDER WHAT IT TAKES TO GO TO HEAVEN.

Many teens mistakenly believe the popular opinion of today that says that heaven is open to pretty much everyone . . . except maybe really evil, wicked people. **Of course, that begs the question: "What constitutes 'evil' or 'wicked?'" In other words, what is the cut-off point? It only makes sense that the cut-off point is sin. And the truth is, only one sin will keep you out of heaven (and most importantly, separated from God).** If you are starting to feel a bit short of breath, don't worry. God provides a way for us to "make the cut" and spend eternity with him. As far as the opinion that heaven is open to most everyone, **Matthew 7:13–14 makes it very clear when it says: "Enter through the narrow gate. For wide is the gate and broad is the road that leads to destruction, and many enter through it. But small is the gate and narrow the road that leads to life, and only a few find it" (NIV).** If you are not sure if you are a Christian, carefully read below what it means to be a follower of Christ. **Remember, this is the most important decision you will ever make in your life.** Read carefully and try to understand what each verse means. Don't worry, we'll take it real slow and go step-by-step.

HEAVEN

WE LEARN ABOUT GOD'S LOVE IN THE BIBLE.

"For God so loved the world that he gave his one and only Son, that whoever believes in him shall not perish but have eternal life." *(John 3:16 NIV)*

God loves you. He wants to bless your life and make it happy, full, and complete. He wants to give you a life that will last forever, even after you die. *Perish* means to die and to be apart from God—forever. God wants you to have "eternal life" in heaven where you are with him forever.

If you understand what John 3:16 means,
put a check here: _____

WE ARE SINFUL.

For all have sinned; all fall short of God's glorious standard. *(Romans 3:23 NLT)*

You may have heard someone say, "I'm only human—nobody's perfect." This Bible verse says the same thing: We are all sinners. No one is perfect. When we sin, we do things that are wrong—things that God would not agree with. The verse says we fall short of "God's glorious standard." Imagine that God gives you a test. Imagine that you have to make a 100 to meet God's "standard." It makes sense that you have to make a 100 because it's a perfect score and God is perfect. Now let's say that everyone starts with a 100, but anytime you sin (do something wrong), you get a point taken off. Since God is perfect and we are not, it is impossible for anyone to make a 100 on this test! I know it sounds like a strict rule, but think about it. If he is holy and perfect, he can't be around people who are not holy and perfect. If he is, he won't be holy and perfect anymore. But before you start to worry that you don't meet his standard (you won't make a 100), just wait—there's good news ahead.

If you understand what Romans 3:23 means, put a check here: _____

SIN HAS A PENALTY (PUNISHMENT).

"For the wages (cost) of sin is death." *(Romans 6:23 NIV)*

Just as criminals must pay the penalty for their crimes, sinners must pay the penalty for their sins. Imagine this: What if every time we do something wrong, we get a ticket (kind of like if you are driving too fast and you get a ticket, and as a punishment you have to pay a penalty). Let's also say that our punishment is not that we have to pay money for our sins, but instead, we have to die. When we die, we will be separated from God for all eternity unless there is a way to pay for our sins (which there is, so don't worry—I'll get to that part). The Bible teaches that those who choose to be separated from God will spend eternity in a place called hell. You may have heard some bad things about hell, but the worst part about hell is that you are in a place where you are separated from God forever.

If you understand what Romans 6:23 means, put a check here: _____

CHRIST HAS PAID THE PRICE FOR OUR SINS!

But God showed his great love for us by sending Christ to die for us while we were still sinners. *(Romans 5:8 NLT)*

The Bible teaches that Jesus Christ, the sinless (perfect) Son of God, has paid the price for all your sins. You may think you have to lead a good life and do good deeds before God will love you. It's good to do good deeds, but it won't pay the price for your sins and get you into heaven. The reason is that no matter how many good deeds you do, you still won't have a 100 (a perfect score). But the Bible says that Christ loved you enough to die for you, even when you were acting unlovable. Pretty amazing, huh?!

If you understand what Romans 5:8 means, put a check here: _____

SALVATION (LIFE IN HEAVEN) IS A FREE GIFT.

God saved you by his special favor when you believed. And you can't take credit for this; it is a gift from God. Salvation is not a reward for the good things we have done, so none of us can boast about it. *(Ephesians 2:8–9 NLT)*

The word *grace* means a gift we don't deserve. It means Christ is offering to pay for something you could never pay for yourself: forgiveness of sins and eternal life, God's gift to you is free. You do not have to work for a gift. That's why it's called a gift. All you have to do is joyfully receive it. Believe with all your heart that Jesus Christ died for you and paid the price for your sins!

If you understand what Ephesians 2:8–9 means, put a check here: _____

CHRIST IS AT YOUR HEART'S DOOR.

"Here I am! I stand at the door and knock. If anyone hears my voice and opens the door, I will come in and eat with him, and he with me."
(Revelation 3:20 NIV)

Jesus Christ wants to have a personal relationship with you. He wants to be your very best friend. He wants you to talk to him just like you would talk to your best friend. Picture, if you will, Jesus Christ standing at the door of your heart and knocking. Invite him in; he is waiting for you to receive him into your heart and life.

If you understand what Revelation 3:20 means, put a check here: _____

YOU MUST RECEIVE HIM.

But to all who believed him and accepted him, he gave the right to become children of God. *(John 1:12 NLT)*

When you receive Christ into your heart you become a child of God, and you can talk to him in prayer at any time about anything. The Christian life is a personal relationship (just like you have with your parents or best friend) with God through Jesus Christ. And best of all, it is a relationship that will last forever and ever. There is nothing you could ever do to make God stop loving you. Even though we will continue to sin from time to time, God still loves us. He never takes his gift back, so we don't have to worry about losing it. It is ours to keep forever.

If you understand what John 1:12 means,
put a check here: _____

So, what do you think about God's offer of forgiveness? **Is this a gift you want to accept? If so, tell God. You don't have to say a fancy prayer—just talk to him and tell him that you believe that Jesus died on the cross for your sins and you want to accept that gift. That's all it takes!** What are you waiting for? Stop and say a prayer right now.

Did you say a prayer and accept God's gift of forgiveness? _____

If you answered "yes," you have an understanding of what it takes to spend eternity with God. Sometimes people say a quick little prayer but never change the course of their lives. They continue along the same path and bank on that little prayer as a sort of "fire insurance" to save them from hell. While it's not my place to say whether or not they are really Christians, *I think we would all agree that if a sincere decision is made to follow Christ, our lives should reflect it.* No, we won't be perfect. Even though Christ has paid the penalty for our sins, we will still blow it from time to time. Our lives should show some evidence of a changed heart. Someone who has made a sincere decision to follow Christ will feel conviction when they sin. They will seek to live a life that is pleasing to God. *In the end, only you know if your decision to follow Christ is a sincere one.* Your primary concern should not be getting to heaven so you can escape hell, but rather to live a life that is pleasing to him *today.* The eternity with God in heaven part is the icing on the cake.

If you did not understand some of the verses above and you still aren't quite sure where you stand when it comes to God's gift of eternal life, please talk to someone who can help you better understand what it means to be a Christian. Maybe it's your pastor, youth minister, parents, or a relative. Maybe it's a friend's mom. *Find someone who knows what it means to be a Christian and tell them you want to know more. It's too important to let the matter go. Better yet, it will change the course of your life forever.* ✳

(Above was adapted from "Your Christian Life" 1965, 1968, as "Aids to Christian Living," 1986 as "Practical Steps in Christian Living," 1995 as "Beginning Your Christian Life," 1997 as "Your Christian Life," Billy Graham Evangelistic Association.)

Crowd over Cross

by Vicki Courtney

If you are a Christian, you know how difficult it can be to choose "the cross" (what God wants you to do) over "the crowd" (what everyone else is doing).

Even Peter, one of Christ's most devoted disciples, denied that he knew Jesus. Jesus had been arrested and was facing crucifixion and Peter denied that he knew Jesus not just once, but three times, and get this . . . to a mere servant girl! Keep in mind, he had witnessed Jesus perform miracle after miracle and traveled everywhere with him as he preached to the crowds, and yet, he had a moment where he chose the crowd over the cross.

Meanwhile, Peter was below in the courtyard. One of the servant girls who worked for the high priest noticed Peter warming himself at the fire. She looked at him closely and then said, "You were one of those with Jesus, the Nazarene." Peter denied it. "I don't know what you're talking about," he said, and he went out in the entryway. Just then, a rooster crowed. The servant girl saw him standing there and began telling the others, "That man is definitely one of them!" Peter denied it again. A little later some other bystanders began saying to Peter, "You must be one of them because you are from Galilee." Peter said, "I swear by God, I don't know this man you're talking about." And immediately the rooster crowed the second time. Suddenly, Jesus' words flashed through Peter's mind: "Before the rooster crows twice, you will deny me three times." And he broke down and cried. (Mark 14:66–72 NLT)

I wish I had given some...

But the story has a happy ending. After Jesus was crucified and arose from the dead, he returned and spoke to the disciples before ascending to heaven. He not only forgave Peter for the denial but gave him the assignment to "feed my sheep." Jesus knew that Peter was truly sorry for the denial. Peter's tears were evidence of his godly sorrow. Because of this, Jesus knew he could trust Peter with a job as important as feeding (taking care of) his sheep (followers). It will be impossible to change our actions unless we have a "godly sorrow" for them. To have *godly sorrow* is to feel sadness over the impact our actions had on God (caused Christ to have to die for our sins). It is not the type of sorrow that comes from being caught. Only godly sorrow will produce true change (repentance) and the ability to choose the cross in the future. Second Corinthians 7:10 (NLT) says, "For God can use sorrow in our lives to help us turn away from sin and seek salvation. We will never regret that kind of sorrow. But sorrow without repentance is the kind that results in death."

The truth is, we will all have moments where we choose the crowd over the cross, and like Peter, will deny our Savior. Just as Jesus forgave and restored Peter, he desires to do the same thing for us. Next time you have a choice to follow the crowd or the cross, remember the sorrow of Peter and more importantly, the love of Christ. Someone who loves us that much is worthy of our allegiance.

When we surveyed girls your age, we asked them to share a time where they chose the crowd over the cross and felt great sorrow. Below is a sampling of their responses. Pay careful attention to *why* many of them felt sorrow. Some mention feeling sorrow because they did something that their parents would be upset about or because it made them "feel bad." While it is a good first step to admit the times where we have chosen the crowd over the cross, remember, a godly sorrow begins with a sorrow to God and a desire to follow him.

When I was with my boyfriend and my friend coming home from Six Flags, it was dark. Well, my friend told me my boyfriend had a surprise for me and it sort of made me nervous. Well, on our way home from Six Flags it was dark and me, my friend, and my boyfriend were sitting in the back of the van. Well, my friend fell asleep on the floor and my boyfriend and I stayed awake. He wanted to make out with me . . . so I did and I regret it because he wasn't worth it and I should have saved that for that special someone.

— *Kathryn, age 13*

At my school if you want to be popular, you have to pretty much be mean and hurt other people's feelings. Well, I gave in and felt really, really bad for hurting a lot of the girls' feelings, so I apologized.

— *Emma, age 12*

I had gone to my friend's house but I didn't know there would be drinking there. Everyone was drinking and my friends convinced me to drink. I was only thirteen at the time. The cops ended up showing up and I got a ticket for minor in consumption. I felt so bad about it.

— *Suzi, age 14*

Last year I went with my neighbor to his friend's house where they were drinking. I told my parents that there wouldn't be any alcohol and I honestly didn't think there would be. I didn't drink at all but I was uncomfortable the entire time I was there. I still haven't told my parents.

— *Kristin, age 16*

It was graduation week. The whole week everyone had been partying. Seniors had been out of school since Friday, prom had been Saturday, and graduation wasn't until Wednesday—we were having fun. I thought, *Oh, it won't hurt for me to go out with everyone. I don't have to drink.* That worked for the first two nights. But you can only resist temptation so long. I ended up giving in. It had been over a month since I had drunk anything; I had been trying to quit. Afterwards I felt horrible, but it couldn't change what I had already done.

— *Amanda, age 18*

The last time I chose "crowd over the cross" was not too long ago. Actually it was graduation night for some of my friends at my old school. I went to a party where there was lots of drinking and smoking. I felt really uncomfortable, but I kept refusing drinks from peers. Then all of a sudden I don't know what happened. I took a drink from my friend and started drinking it.

I really regret doing it now. I try really hard to make decisions to go places where I would not have the pressures of drinking. Thank you so much for giving me the opportunity to confess that. (Editor's note: No problem! But more importantly, confess it to the Lord if you haven't done so already.)

— *Tiffany, age 17*

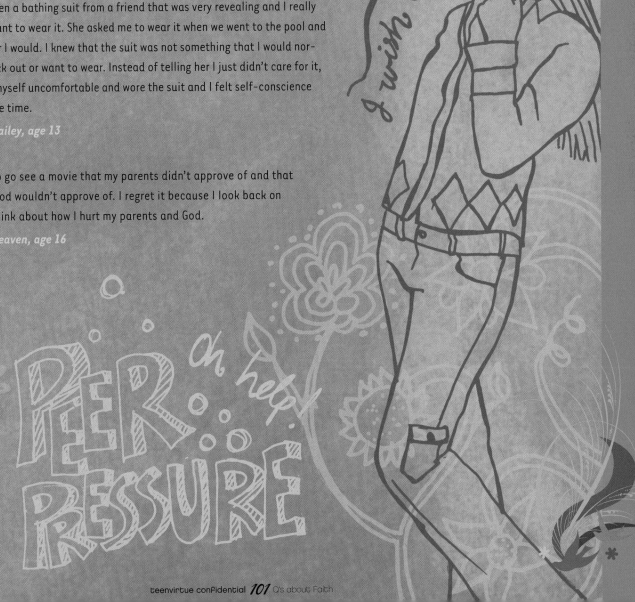

I wish I hadn't worn that.

I was given a bathing suit from a friend that was very revealing and I really didn't want to wear it. She asked me to wear it when we went to the pool and I told her I would. I knew that the suit was not something that I would normally pick out or want to wear. Instead of telling her I just didn't care for it, I made myself uncomfortable and wore the suit and I felt self-conscience the whole time.

— *Hailey, age 13*

I went to go see a movie that my parents didn't approve of and that I know God wouldn't approve of. I regret it because I look back on it and think about how I hurt my parents and God.

— *Heaven, age 16*

PEER
Oh, help!
PRESSURE

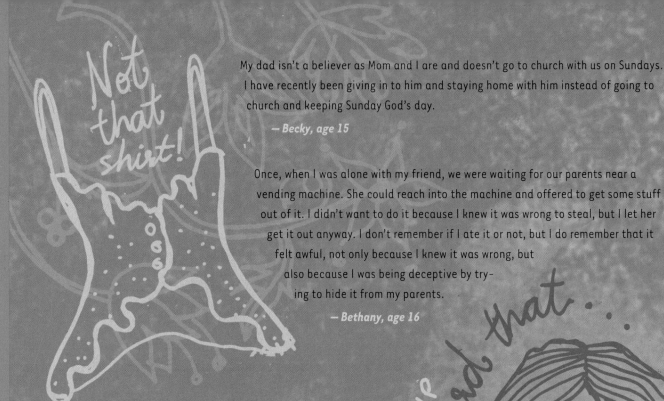

Not that shirt!

My dad isn't a believer as Mom and I are and doesn't go to church with us on Sundays. I have recently been giving in to him and staying home with him instead of going to church and keeping Sunday God's day.

— *Becky, age 15*

Once, when I was alone with my friend, we were waiting for our parents near a vending machine. She could reach into the machine and offered to get some stuff out of it. I didn't want to do it because I knew it was wrong to steal, but I let her get it out anyway. I don't remember if I ate it or not, but I do remember that it felt awful, not only because I knew it was wrong, but also because I was being deceptive by trying to hide it from my parents.

— *Bethany, age 16*

My friends told me to wear a shirt that was very revealing and I wore it. I knew I shouldn't and plus I didn't feel comfortable wearing it.

— *Trudi, age 13*

I have a really good friend who has been friends with me since we were four. Well, I didn't realize that she was such a good friend until the second semester of our freshman year. I had this other group of friends who weren't very nice and when my friend would come talk to me, they would talk bad about her as soon as she left. Well, not wanting to lose my new found "great" friends, I joined in and trashed this girl who had always been there for me and always had my back. I now realize how bad this group of friends is and how important my lifelong friend is.

— *Meagan, age 14*

Gossip Gossip Gossip Gossip I wish I hadn't heard that . . .

When my friends were all getting boyfriends, I wanted one. My mom said I wasn't allowed to have one until I was sixteen years old. A guy named Jimmy asked me out, and I said yes. Later, my mom found out and she made me break up with him. She wanted us to just be friends. I regretted dating him because it broke my heart to hurt his feelings.

— *Bethany, age 13*

I am a very naturally joyful person, but last year the most popular guy in my grade told me that I smiled too much and that he disliked how often I laughed. I literally stopped smiling for three months, and I regret that SO much now, because I see so many lost opportunities that I could have had to be joyful and make an impact on someone else! After those miserable three months, I realized that my joy is in Christ, and no one's opinion should keep me from reflecting that joy!

— *Julie, age 14*

I was at a sleepover at one of my friend's houses and of course, we were talking about what girls usually talk about at sleepovers. Unfortunately, in a lot of cases, this means some sort of gossip is going to pop up. Well it did. Even though I wasn't saying all the juicy stuff, I was listening to it. That's just as bad. The Holy Spirit was tugging at me, and he recalled to my mind when someone told me listening to gossip is just as bad as saying it. I ignored it and my selfish desire to hear it won over.

— **Rebecca, age 15**

I earn a fairly large income being a nanny for a family of three children several days a week. Having gone to church all my life, I know that God wants me to tithe regularly, but last month I conveniently "forgot." My jealousy overrode the voice of my conscience, reminding me of what God has asked, and instead convinced me it would be OK to skip tithing juuuust this once. So I did, and now I regret it.

— *Laurel, age 17*

SHADOW

BLACK NAIL

BLACK

My dark life...

I would have to say the last time I chose the crowd over the cross would be when it came down to the guys I dated. Where I live, it is a big thing to have a boyfriend. I wanted to fit in and I also wanted the kind of attention you get from having a boyfriend, so I started looking for a suitable Christian guy. I looked for about a year and couldn't find one, so I decided that the guy I dated didn't need to be a Christian. I just wanted to have a boyfriend. It didn't take me long to find a non-Christian guy. He smoked, drank alcohol, played with weapons, had anger management problems, he was hateful to most people, did drugs, and quite a bit more. We dated for four months without letting my parents know. I became real popular with my friends because I had finally found a boyfriend. The one set back was my relationship with my parents. We started arguing a lot more than normal. I started growing rebellious. Once I saw how much more my friends liked me because I was dating this guy I decided that they might like me even more if I went Goth. I started wearing all black and watching things on the computers at school that I knew I shouldn't be watching. I listened to the spells some of my friends would say and I would repeat them for fun. During this time things only got worse with my parents. It was a hard time. Finally I realized that all of the problems in my life were caused by me and the things I had chosen to do. I knew what I had to do, but I didn't want to do it. I had to tell my parents about the guy and to quit being rebellious. Once I let those changes take place in my life, things got a whole lot easier.

— *Ashlee, age 15*

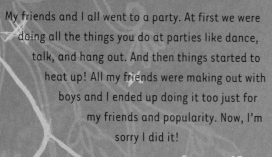

My friends and I all went to a party. At first we were doing all the things you do at parties like dance, talk, and hang out. And then things started to heat up! All my friends were making out with boys and I ended up doing it too just for my friends and popularity. Now, I'm sorry I did it!

— Sara, age 13

Why did I steal that?

I fell under the "power" of peer pressure and I stole something from PetCo. But, I felt so bad that the next day I went back and spent all of my money to make up for it. (Editor's Note: I know this is radical, but true repentance means taking the item back and talking to a Manager. Offer to pay for the item. Depending on the value of the item, most managers won't press charges, but it's the right thing to do.)

— Grace, age 12

Once when I was with my friends we decided to play truth or dare and even though I knew it was wrong to kiss someone I didn't have feelings for, I chose the crowd over the cross. I gave into peer pressure and the panic of "never

sorry

turning down a dare." I regret this because even though it was only a kiss; I feel like I gave away part of my heart to someone who I barely know.

— Becca, age 16

When I was fifteen, my parents went through a divorce. I was visiting with my dad and his girlfriend for Thanksgiving and we went to my dad's sister's house. After the younger kids were put to bed they let the two teenage girls stay up. They offered us a wine cooler and I accepted it, so that my dad would accept me. I have since regretted that decision and God has forgiven me for it. (Editor's Note: Ugh! That's what we call irresponsible parenting! You sound like a very mature girl. Keep your eyes on Jesus and maybe it will rub off on your dad, someday!)

— Brooklynne, age 17 *

I AM FORGIVEN

weigh in @ virtuous reality .com

Survey: Crossover Crowd

Here's the part of the survey where we asked girls your age to share about a time where they chose "the cross" over "the crowd." It warmed my heart to hear about the stand so many girls your age are taking for Christ. I hope that these examples will inspire you as much as they inspired me. Most of all, know that you are not alone out there! There are many girls your age facing the same pressures and temptations you do and deciding to choose the cross over the crowd. Remember that the next time you feel like you're the only one taking a stand and choosing the cross.

I was at school when my friend asked me if I wanted to go to a PG13 movie with her and her older sisters, but my mom had signed me up for a church retreat. At the time I thought it was really lame. After thinking about it for a week and getting bugged by my friends, I decided to go to the retreat because something was telling me deep inside my gut to go. I ended up becoming a Christian at the retreat!

— Suzanne, age 12

Sometimes at school it seems like it's all about being in the right "group" at lunch. One day there was a girl and she was sitting all by herself and she just kept glancing over at us, so I went and sat with her. We have been close friends ever since.

— Michele, age 14

On a school trip, our group went to the mall. We separated into smaller groups, and mine decided to go into a store called Spencer's. I had never been there before and had no idea what it contained. I quickly discovered that its products were most certainly not of God. Instead of staying in the store with them, I chose to wait outside on a bench until they were finished looking. It was hard to sit by myself, but it was worth it.

— *Koriann, age 17*

I was at a school dance party and I thought the dancing was bad. My friends also agreed with me. There were parents there but they did not seem to care. When I finally noticed that the grown-ups wouldn't come to the rescue, I called my mom and left the party.

— *Grace, age 14*

About a week ago I was offered a job at Abercrombie & Fitch so I prayed about it and asked my parents to also pray about it. We came to the understanding that this was where God wanted me to be. My friends and leaders in my church asked to my face and behind my back, "How can the youth minister's daughter work at Abercrombie?" They make jokes and bash me up and down. But right now I'm praying for the salvation of every person I work with and praying that I would be a light to them in any way I can. Yesterday a coworker told me, "Laura, I want to go to church with you." And of course, I invited her! Understand that I do not agree with the way Abercrombie does their business, but I do agree with Jesus when he said it's not the healthy who need a doctor, but the sick.

— *Laura, age 18*

There was a time when I was at a slumber party with my cheerleading squad and they really wanted to watch a movie that I knew I couldn't watch. I was the youngest member on the squad and I felt kind of intimidated, but I gathered up enough courage to tell them I couldn't watch it. They respected me for it and we didn't watch it, no questions asked. In fact, one of my friends on the squad thanked me later and apologized for not being the one to say something.

— *Laura, age 17*

I chose to lead a Bible study for my non-Christian friends instead of socializing during my lunch period.

— *Kristina, age 15*

Well, there was this pool party. I knew there were going to be guys there. Almost all the girls were wearing bikinis. I chose to wear a more modest swimsuit. I also wore some cute shorts over it.

— *Carin, age 13*

I have been asked by people to go to parties where there would be drinking and I declined, knowing that it was not right.

— *Kara, age 17*

There was this new girl in school and she came from Thailand and didn't speak English. All these kids were making fun of her because they would ask a question and she would speak Thai. I asked her to sit at my table and walked her to her classes. Now we sit together at lunch!

— *Renee, age 14*

Some people were openly cheating in social studies on a test and I refused to join in.

— *Kimmi, age 14*

I played basketball in tenth grade, and I had to run twenty laps around the gym every Wednesday so that I could leave practice early and go to church for the Wednesday night youth service.

— *Sarah, age 18*

We were watching a movie that I knew wasn't good to watch so I asked to be excused from class.

— *Cristale, age 15*

Well, I got invited to this party and I knew there was going to be drinking. Most of my friends were going, but I still said no. A whole bunch of people ended up getting drunk and a few had sex.

— *Kinsey, age 15*

One of my non-Christian friends was jogging with me and she was telling me how her friend's mom wasn't home last weekend and how they invited some people to her house and had a little party. One of the boys brought vodka. She continued with her story and said her friend got caught and extremely grounded. It was hard for me to think of what to say, so I didn't say anything. She continued to talk, explaining that she drank . . . I immediately opened my mouth and told her drinking as a thirteen-year-old is illegal, she could go to jail. She just blew it off. I have been friends with her since first grade, and now I think God is telling me we are going down different paths . . . I thought I could change her by bringing her to church, but it never worked. It will be hard for me to let that friendship go, but God just showed me that if I continue to hang around people like that, I too will be in a situation where I might choose the crowd-drinking party. God just gave me a wake up call, and I think I finally woke up.

— *Allison, age 13*

Once I was with a group of friends who wanted to steal something. They wanted me to also, but I just walked away.

— *Kayla, age 15*

I was at school and there was a boy who had stolen my Bible. I asked him to give it back, but he wouldn't. He said he would give it back if I said a phrase I knew I shouldn't say. The only reason he was trying to get me to say it was because he knew I was a Christian and he had never heard me say it before. He also said if I didn't say it he would take my Bible home and I probably wouldn't see it again. I didn't say it and after we both left class, we were walking down the hallway and just as we were going separate ways he handed me my Bible!

— *Hannah, age 16*

At lunch usually most of my friends don't do their homework so they just cheat. A lot! They always ask me for my work and I'm pressured to give it to them but I remember that God's Word says not to cheat and to always do the right thing. And even though sometimes it's hard, I usually manage to stick it out.

— *Raegan, age 14*

Two of my friends are boyfriend and girlfriend. One day when we were all at a get-together and we were playing video games and the two of them started acting inappropriately affectionate, and I told them they should stop.

— *Emily, age 13*

A few friends and I were going to see a movie, and when we got there the only one that was showing was rated R for sexual content, language, and violence. They went in, I went home.

— *Chelsi, age 17*

Cheating has been and is a big issue in my high school. So far, when the temptation is there, I haven't copied homework assignments or cheated on tests, even when that means getting a lower grade than people cheating. I put a higher value on my character than my GPA. I also won't accept burned CDs or download music illegally, even though I have friends willing to let me copy their music.

— *Alyssa, age 17*

One time during lunch, my friend, Jenny, asked me if I was a virgin. I replied, "Yes, aren't you?" And she said, "No." My friend Carlos came over and Jenny asked him the same question. He replied of course that it would be wrong to cheat on his future wife. Jenny said that being a virgin was stupid and you never get to do anything fun with guys. I disagreed with her and told her why it was important.

— *Jasmine, age 14*

My freshman year I would eat alone instead of eating with my friends from middle school because they were into the whole party/sex scene.

— *Katie, age 17*

On New Year's Eve people who I thought were my friends decided to get drunk and flirt with these older guys. I decided to hang out with my parents and their friends and watch the fireworks.

— *Samantha, age 16*

Just last week, I missed the announcement at school that the next morning students were invited to the flagpole right outside of the school to pray and worship God. The next morning as my bus pulled up to the school doors, I saw about twenty to thirty kids around the flagpole. My non-Christian friends on the bus made some cruel comments about how the lame kids around the flagpole were idiots to get up this early and "pray to a god who doesn't exist." I turned to the people on the bus and said, "I'm going to join them. Do you want to come with me?" They declined my offer and watched me join the "lame" kids around the flagpole.

— *Becky, age 15*

Almost everybody on my softball team was excited about getting their nickname written across the back of their softball shorts. There was me and another girl who said we wouldn't wear them if we got them because we didn't want guys to look at us in that spot.

— *Natalie, age 15*

Instead of going to drinking parties after prom, I'm going to spend time with a couple of my good friends from church.

— *Rebecca, age 17*

When I was a cheerleader at my middle school, all the girls would cuss and talk bad about other people. It was really hard not to join in with them because some of the stuff they said was true, but it still wasn't right. I asked God to help me because I didn't want to get a bad reputation. At the end of the season I was glad I didn't fall into temptation.

— *Kirsten, age 14*

I was at volleyball training and we played a teambuilding game. Most of the girls danced immodestly, so I asked the coach if I could sit out.

— *Gabbi, age 16*

I was on a really good volleyball team and we were about to start tournaments. It consisted of missing four Sundays in a row, so I said I would have to decline.

— *Ashton, age 17*

I go to a private Christian school that promotes modesty. We have an awards ceremony at the end of the year, however, and all the girls go hog wild and wear strapless dresses and the like. This year I found a gorgeous little black dress that made me look beautiful. It was strapless, however, and the cut drew attention to my chest. I wanted it so much, but my parents said I couldn't have it. It took me a while, but soon I accepted it and found a simpler dress to wear. I followed the "modest cross" rather than the "strapless crowd."

— *Louisa, age 14*

I have never been a fan of secular pop music . . .
I avoided Brittney Spears, rap, and any other
music that may contain provocative lyrics
because I do not want to be singing along with
the negative message. I listen to all the lyrics on a CD of an artist—Christian,
Disney, and most Country are
the music genres for me!!!

— *Alicia, age 16*

When my friends and I were playing a simple game of truth or dare (like
chewing on a pinecone—don't ask), they dared me
to flash people or pole dance and I didn't do either, even
though they really pressured me and got mad when I didn't do it.

— **Leah, age 13**

After a basketball game, some girls chose to take some things from the other team's lost and
found. I told them that it was wrong and they shouldn't do it and I left the locker room. They
ended up taking stuff anyway and got caught. Later one of the girls came and told me she
wished she wouldn't have taken the items.

— **Koby, age 14**

In English we're reading a book that takes God's name in vain a whole lot, and we have to read
out loud. My teacher asked who had a problem with reading it out loud and I was the only one
who refused to do it.

— **Katherine, age 17**

One time in my choir class we had a day when we brought our favorite song and some of the girls
started dancing inappropriately in front of some guys. They told me to join in but I told them
I wouldn't. They made fun of me by saying I couldn't dance but I knew it wasn't right.

— **Lauren, age 13**

I was IMing one day, and one of my guy friends started asking me questions about his exgirl-
friend. He wanted to know if I thought she was snobby and stuff. So instead of answering, I just
said, "I'm actually trying not to gossip about my friends."

— **Stephanie, age 15**

At a sleepover with two of my best friends, they started to watch a movie that had
a lot of cussing and junk. Instead of staying there I went into the living room and
watched regular TV. I was glad I did, too, because I later found out that the Bible
says to guard our hearts! In other words don't pollute it with bad words or anything
that God would not approve of.

— **Jamie, age 12** *

weigh in
@
virtuous
reality
.com

YOUR QUESTIONS ABOUT FAITH

by Susie Davis
+ Susan Jones
+ Vicki Courtney

#1. What is HEAVEN like?

by Susie Davis

One way to understand heaven is to read the book of Revelation, which is the last book in the Bible. Revelation contains many symbols that describe heaven in addition to letting us know what will take place in heaven itself. I encourage you to read it yourself and see what you think. Keep in mind that many brilliant theologians have attempted to dissect and understand Revelation resulting in many opinions about what exactly God is getting at regarding the timing and the symbolism in the book of Revelation. It is quite fascinating and sometimes a little confusing for me. Now, while Revelation requires stretching your imagination to get your mind around the whole heaven thing, **there is a simpler and more understandable picture of heaven presented in the Bible by Jesus himself. It is the one I turn to when I am trying to understand what heaven will be like.** It is also the picture I remember when someone I love dies. When someone you know dies, it is natural to try and understand what is going to happen to them. Death can bring up so many questions and the thought of heaven can actually become a comfort in itself for those who grieve. Let's look at what Jesus said about heaven by starting with some key verses to get a biblical picture.

Jesus says, "Do not let your hearts be troubled. Trust in GOD. Trust also in ME."

John 14:1–4 tells us (and this is Jesus speaking), "Do not let your hearts be troubled. Trust in God; trust also in me. In my Father's house are many rooms; if it were not so, I would have told you. I am going there to prepare a place for you. And if I go and prepare a place for you, I will come back and take you to be with me that you also may be where I am. You know the way to the place where I am going" (NIV).

These verses describe two key facts. **One is that we don't need to worry about heaven and the stuff that will happen to us when we are there.** If we trust God, then we can know with certainty that Jesus prepares a place for us. So no worrying about being left out or forgotten when Jesus is the one holding the spot. It's just like when you hear your mom calling out that dinner is ready—you don't creep into the dining room and wonder if there is a place set for you. No, instead you walk in with no worries at all that there will be a place at the table, your place, and no one else will be taking it. In the same way, Jesus reassures us that if we have trusted him, then there are no concerns about our spot in heaven. That is comforting.

The other point in the verse above is that there is actually a house—God's house. Now I'm not too sure about what God's house is like, but I like the idea that he has one and I'm invited in. In addition, I imagine that in God's house I'll feel like I am at home. Not like staying in some gross hotel where the sheets are questionably clean or the mattress is hard and painful to sleep on. Or a place that makes my eyes tired taking in all the newness—instead, I imagine that I will feel as though I have finally arrived at the place I have been longing for and couldn't quite understand.

Psalm 90:1 states, "Lord, through all the generations you have been our home!" (NLT). I really love that verse because it is saying that God himself is our home. Imagine it this way: think to a time when you were gone on a long vacation or away at camp. Let's say after a while you had your fill of sightseeing and entertainment, so all you really wanted was just to go home and sleep in your own bed. Go home and cozy up with your favorite book on your own chair in your own house. Home . . . the word itself speaks of peace and comfort. Well, just like your house reflects its owners, heaven itself will mirror God because it is his home. **And the reason that we will love heaven is because we love God. God is what the deep down part of our spirit is always longing for.** So when we get to heaven, there we will be encapsulated in God himself . . . in his house . . . surrounded by all things God and that will be the best homecoming we have ever experienced. It will be . . . heaven.

#2. How can a loving God let people go to HELL? And what about those who haven't even heard about CHRIST?

by Susie Davis

First, let's start by looking at a verse about God's intentions where all people are concerned because **God doesn't desire that anyone should go to hell, rather that all should come to know him as Lord. 2 Peter 3:9 states, "The Lord isn't slow about keeping his promises, as some people think he is. In fact, God is patient, because he wants everyone to turn from sin and no one to be lost" (CEV).** God wants people to choose him. But the fact is that from the beginning he has

Free to Choose or Reject...

allowed us to make our own choices—even if we are the ones that ultimately break his heart. **When God established that humans would have freedom of choice, he risked that many would use the freedom to reject him.** And the rejection of Jesus is a choice to be separated from God for all eternity. And so at this point you might argue that God should compel us to choose heaven over hell. And the truth is that he could have done it that way but he didn't because he loves us. **We aren't robotic beings under a dictatorship; rather, we are free will beings under a loving sovereignty. The fact that God is sovereign means that he makes the rules.** The rules in this case mean making a decision this side of eternity for Christ will equal an eternity with Christ in heaven. **So in answer to how could God allow . . . God allows because he loves.**

I imagine the second question is more about the native on the island who has never heard the

news about Jesus Christ, right? Romans 1:19–20 provides the answer to this question. It says, **"For the truth about God is known to them instinctively. God has put this knowledge in their hearts. From the time the world was created, people have seen the earth and sky and all that God made. They can clearly see his invisible qualities—his eternal power and divine nature. So they have no excuse whatsoever for not knowing God"** (NLT). Another paraphrase called *The Message* says it this way, "But the basic reality of God is plain enough. Open your eyes and there it is! By taking a long and thoughtful look at what God has created, people have always been able to see what their eyes as such can't see: eternal power, for instance, and the mystery of his divine being. So nobody has a good excuse."

Basically what the verse means is that the reality of God is made known through creation or nature. It contends the invisible qualities of eternal power and divine nature are evidence for a holy God. **While this might be hard for you to imagine—** and we could debate endlessly about the perceived relevance of the verse—we will all either choose to believe it or not.

the reality of GOD is made known through CREATION.

#3. How can I become totally ON FIRE for GOD?

by Susie Davis

Wow! I love this. Can you imagine the way God feels knowing you are asking this question? I imagine it makes him smile. Desiring to live wholeheartedly and passionately for God is such an admirable goal. It seems to me that there are some basic things to know about how to live a fervent life for God but by giving you how to steps, I feel I would be misleading you. **For one, a fired up passion for God equals a genuine love for him.** And a genuine love for God is a little hard to nail down, much less manufacture.

There are so many people in the Bible that I feel that obviously manifest the zeal for God. By looking at them maybe we can gather some clues. For example, let's look at King David in the Old Testament. He was called a man after God's own heart. He is definitely someone that I would say was on fire for God. When I read about his life, I can clearly see his love for God manifested in his actions and his writing (he is credited with authoring most of the psalms). So I have to ask myself, *What was it about David that created that fire?* It was his love for God. Then I look at Mary in the New Testament who anointed Christ's head with oil, risking (and receiving) ridicule from the men around her. Christ indicated she was an example to follow. And I ask again, *What was it about her that created the fire?* It was her love for God. I think about Paul and his unrelenting devotion to Jesus as manifested by his work for the church. And I wonder what was it about Paul? Again, it was that he loved Christ. All this leads me to tell you that being on fire for God is much more about an individual out pouring of love for Jesus than any single action we could perform.

In Philippians 3:8 Paul gets at the heart of it by writing this, **"Nothing is as wonderful as knowing Christ Jesus my Lord. I have given up everything else and count it all as garbage. All I want is Christ"** (cev). That is a man in love with his God. It is abandonment to Christ, ranking Christ as the most supreme piece of life. Clearly Paul's internal motivation for everything he did—all those "fired up" actions were really just a wholehearted love and desire for God. Pure and simple. I want that kind of love for God and no doubt you do too. So how to love God more? Just ask. I do. I ask God all the time to help me love him more. I pray daily, *Lord, help me to love you all my life with all my energy.* I don't want to be a Christian that gets wrapped up in the garbage of life and honestly, without God's help, I know that I could. So I ask and I ask and I ask. And he in return becomes more and more the object of my devotion.

Lord, help me to love You.

#4. How come God seems so FAR AWAY? I want to get closer to Him, but I don't know how.

by Susie Davis

Let me tell you, I could have submitted this question just this week. It seems to be an especially quiet time in my life where God is concerned. Just know that your feelings are normal and many Christians* feel like you and I do from time to time. **While it is normal to feel as though God is far away, you need to remember that he is not. God is close to you whether you feel he is or not—why, if you are a Christian, his very Spirit lives within you!** That's the great news. But if just reminding yourself of that fact doesn't quite do it for you, let me share some of the ways I pull into God when I am feeling far from him.

actively listen for God

• **Start by looking at your life realistically and see if you are actively listening for God.** Listening to God is something that you need to begin practicing on a regular basis. One of the best ways to hear from God is by reading the Bible. The words in the Bible are God's inspired story written just for you and me. **Psalm 119:105 tells us, "Your word is a lamp for my feet and a light for my path" (NLT).** Reading the Bible is a way of turning on your spiritual ears or lighting a way for spiritual sight. If you aren't in the habit of reading the Bible, it could honestly be very difficult to feel like God is talking to you. The words in the Bible are meant to provide direction for your life and comfort in hard times. There have been many times when I have gone to bed praying over a problem, wondering if God heard me at all, only to wake up in the morning, sit down and read the Bible, and find the exact answer I needed. Listening to God also includes prayer. Although we often only make prayer about asking for things, prayer can be a time of listening to God too. **Sitting still long enough to read the Bible and pray often results in feeling closer to God. Another way to get close to God is by going to church.** Singing songs to God in worship and listening to godly, biblical teachers creates an awareness of God's closeness. These are the things you can input in your life to posture yourself as a listener. Make sure that you are doing those things if you want to hear from and experience nearness to God.

*A Christian is someone who has asked Jesus Christ to be the Lord and Savior of their life. For more information read the articles entitled, "A Leap of Faith" and "The Scoop on . . . Heaven."

• **Next, ask yourself if you are in a season of intentional sin against God.** If you are willingly and consciously doing things that you know God hates, then you are grieving God. In Ephesians 4:30, *The Message* says it this way, "Don't grieve God. Don't break his heart. His Holy Spirit, moving and breathing in you, is the most intimate part of your life, making you fit for himself. Don't take such a gift for granted." When we do things that make the Holy Spirit sad, God can seem silent—much like how you feel when someone hurts your feelings.

• **Finally, know God isn't trying to hide himself from you.** He isn't too busy or waiting on perfect performance to speak to you. One of my favorite verses is **James 4:8 that says, "Draw near to God and He will draw near to you"** (HCSB). I love the idea that if I am trying to get close to God, God will get close to me. This is so reassuring. It means that we can rest in the knowledge that even while we actively draw toward God (like for example, doing the things mentioned above) even if we don't feel especially close to him—we can know that he is pulling near to us. Another verse says it a bit differently. It is another promise about what happens when we genuinely desire God. **Psalm 145:18 states, "The Lord is close to all who call on him, yes, to all who call on him sincerely"** (NLT). Both of these verses confirm the fact that if God is true to his Word—and he always is—then we can be assured that he is close to us even when we feel otherwise.

draw near to God and He will draw near to you.

#5. How can I talk to my non-Christian FRIENDS about Christ without them getting MAD at me?
by Susan Jones & Vicki Courtney

St. Francis of Assisi once said, **"Preach the gospel at all times. Use words when necessary."**[1] That statement is a great way to communicate how our lives should be "living sermons" to others. **John 13:34 says, "So now I am giving you a new commandment: Love each other. Just as I have loved you, you should love each other"** (NLT).

Wow. That's a tall order. Initially, the command was to love others as you love yourself (see Leviticus 19:18 and Romans 13:9). Now, let's face it. We're all a tad egocentric (some more than others), so it's easy to love ourselves, but much more difficult to apply that degree of love to others. But then Jesus takes it up another notch and tells us to love others as HE loves us. Wow, again.

"Preach the Gospel at all times. Use words if necessary."
— St. Francis of Assisi

If you make it your aim to love your friends like Jesus loves you, before long, they will begin to notice something different about you. It is NOT normal to put others' needs and desires above your own. Let your life speak as an example. **I've never known people to get mad over someone loving them with the love of Christ.** St. Francis was a wise man to recognize that our actions and love toward others will have a greater impact than our words.

Matthew 28:19–20 commands us to "go and make disciples of all nations . . . and teaching them to obey everything I have commanded you" (NIV). This charge is known as "the Great Commission." According to this verse, it is our duty to talk to our non-Christian friends about Jesus Christ. You are to be admired for your obedience to the task God has given you. Don't lose hope when you are met with ridicule and anger. Keep pressing on.

Here are a few tips you can follow when talking to your friends about God and your Christian faith.

*1. Be humble.

Approach the subject with humility, not with a know-it-all attitude that says, "I'm right and you're wrong." This is very important. People do not respond well to know-it-alls. If you act like you're better than them, then they will probably not respect you enough to listen to what you have to say. In fact, many will become defensive and be focused more on how to match your tone and argue back.

*2. Listen.

Listen to what they have to say. It doesn't mean you have to agree with it, but it will give you a good idea of where they are coming from. You might be able to determine why they get angry when you talk about God. Many people who are defensive about Christianity have had a bad experience with "Christians behaving badly" at some point in their lives. If they share a valid disappointment, reply with empathy and tell them how sorry you are that they were left with a bad representation of the Christian faith. Make a point to tell them that Christians are humans and humans are prone to sin. Tell them to look directly to Jesus for the sincerest example of Christianity.

*3. Pray for opportunities to slip it into natural conversation.

Ask God to give you opportunities where it would be natural for you to talk about your faith. For instance, perhaps you've just studied about the theory of evolution in biology. You could ask your friends what they think after class.

*4. Speak from your own personal experience.

It is impossible to argue with someone about a real-life experience someone has had. Share about your own personal relationship with Christ. When the opportunity presents itself, talk about answered prayers or how God has helped you through a tough challenge.

*5. Invite them to church, Christian events and concerts, or Christian organizations at your school.

It's hard to turn down a fun event, and often times all they need is an invitation. **If they witness other people their age who are following Christ, they may be more receptive to it.**

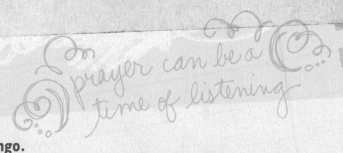

*6. Lay off the Christian lingo.

Using phrases like "sanctified, born-again, and saved" can be a bit overwhelming to someone who doesn't have a clue what you are talking about. Also, try not to use the word "lost" when referring to non-Christians. **Remember, they don't see themselves as "lost" and would be insulted if someone called them that.**

*7. Don't feel like you have to have all the answers.

It's OK to say, "I don't really know the answer to that" if they ask you a tough question. Tell them you will talk to your pastor or youth minister and see what they have for an answer. They may not have an answer either and **there is nothing wrong with telling them that there are some questions we will not have answers for this side of heaven.**

*8. Focus on your sins . . . not theirs.

If your conversations about Christianity always center around their sin and need of Christ, they are likely going to tune you out or get defensive. This is a tricky balance because they will have to acknowledge their sin before they can see Christ as the solution, but they are not likely to do so if they feel attacked and accused. Try focusing on your own shortcomings and how Christ's forgiveness has impacted your life. Don't be afraid to share your weaknesses and areas of your life where you have asked Christ to help you improve.

*9. Don't give up on them.

Never cease praying for them. Your example or spoken words may have an impact on their coming to Christ years down the road.

*10. Leave the results to God.

You never know what God is doing in the heart of another person. Only he can bring them to salvation. Even if they become a Christian as a result of your example or encouraging words, **God did the work—not you. As Christians, we should never forget this. ✶**

---

[1] See: http://en.thinkexist.com/quotes/st._francis_of_assisi.

SURVEY: ONLINE STRANGERS

BY VICKI COURTN

The Internet is here to stay.
By now, you've probably experienced
the unpleasant experience of being
contacted by a stranger online. How do I know?
You told us in a survey our ministry conducted
with middle and high school girls. In the survey,
we asked girls if they had ever been contacted by
a stranger and if so, to describe what happened.
We then asked if they had told their parents about
it. I have done hundreds of interviews with radio
stations, newspapers, and even television shows
on the subject of Internet safety, so I am more
than aware of the statistic that one in five kids
online has been solicited for sex. However, nothing prepared me for how many of you had actually
been contacted by a stranger and had some pretty
creepy stories to tell.

**Social networking
sites like MySpace
have made it easy
for predators and
other weirdos to
target preteens and
teens who inno-**

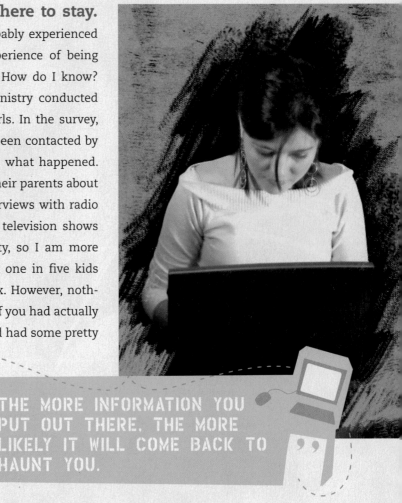

> THE MORE INFORMATION YOU
> PUT OUT THERE, THE MORE
> LIKELY IT WILL COME BACK TO
> HAUNT YOU.

cently share too much information. Many will
pretend to be your age and claim to have some
of the same interests in order to gain your trust.
Would you believe that there are more than

990 million people who have access to the
Internet? Nothing you ever post is really private.
And it's not just predators and creeps who are

YOUR SCARY STORIES

looking at your information, but also colleges and employers. I am reading more and more articles about colleges and employers researching MySpace, Facebook, and other sites for background on potential students or potential employees. I say "potential" because many are not being accepted are hired as a result of their pages.

The more information you put out there, the more likely it will come back to haunt you. When my son got his roommate assignment for college, he found enough information on Facebook to cause us to pick up the phone and call the college to request a change. Now, do you think this guy ever imagined that a random assigned roommate and his entire family would be looking at his page and pictures? Probably not! **So, how do we solve this problem of sharing too much information? Think before you type! Here are some tips to remember:**

→ **NEVER** share your last name, city, or school name. (Exceptions are when you are in a school network like Facebook.)

→ **NEVER** share your e-mail, cell phone number, or screen name. Basically, don't give anyone a way to contact you one-on-one.

→ **BE CAREFUL** about what pictures you post. Even silly provocative poses can be misread by others to mean something else. Don't ever post pictures in your swimsuit, undergarments, or pajamas.

→ **REMOVE INAPPROPRIATE COMMENTS** made by others. Remember, many will judge you based on these comments and assume "guilt by association."

→ Most important, **SET YOUR PAGE TO PRIVATE OR JOIN AS FEW NETWORKS AS POSSIBLE!** Most predators and weirdos will not go to the trouble to send a friend request

"REMOVE INAPPROPRIATE COMMENTS MADE BY OTHERS. MANY WILL JUDGE YOU BASED ON THESE COMMENTS AND ASSUME "GUILT BY ASSOCIATION.""

especially when there are so many other pages that are open to the public. It is like adding a lock to your door. It's not 100 percent effective, but it certainly helps.

→ **TELL YOUR PARENTS if someone contacts you and makes you feel uncomfortable.** I realize that many of you are afraid your parents will freak out and shut down your page or ground you from the Internet, but you have to involve an adult if you are in danger. At the very least, go to *www.cybertipline. com* and copy and paste the offensive comments/solicitation and e-mail it to them.

This random guy sent me an e-mail. I don't know how he got my address, but I kind of freaked out when I saw that I had a message from someone I didn't know. It was in my bulk folder, so I immediately deleted it. I told my best friend, and she said that it had happened to her once before and gave the name of the person who had e-mailed her. It was the same guy. She was curious and read the email. She said it said something about him being seventeen (we were in sixth or seventh grade) and wanting to be her friend. She was scared that he was stalking her. I told her not to read any more e-mails from him, and even sent him an e-mail telling him, "Don't ever e-mail me again, I don't know you." I haven't gotten a message from him since, and I don't think my friend has either. I didn't tell my parents, however, because I thought they'd get mad at me (they didn't know I had a Xanga, and I was scared they'd find out and make me stop it, but I ended up stopping it anyway).
— *Deidre, age 14*

Yes, I have. Random people contact me on MySpace every now and then and they ask to be my friend or ask questions about where I live and such. I don't respond to someone I don't recognize on MySpace. And yes, I did tell my mom.
— *Laura, age 18*

Yes, I have, especially on MySpace. I get messages and friend invites all the time and things that say, "You're hot" and stuff. I usually look at their page and see if I know them, and if I don't, then I send them a message asking how they know me. If I have no clue who they are and they are just a random person then I avoid and end all contact with that person. And no, I don't usually tell my parents about it. *(Editor's Note: MySpace automatically sets your page to private if you list your age as fourteen or fifteen, so you must be lying about your age. There is no reason to have your page open to the public! Set it to private and it will cut down on the number of weirdos contacting you.)*

— *Ashley, age 14*

Yes, I have had a stranger contact me online. They told me they went to my school and somehow they knew what school I went to. They didn't know my name, which was a good thing. I told them I had to go and they were like no don't go . . .so I said hold on . . . and I went to get my mom. It was really scary.

— *Chelsea, age 14*

I have people contact me online all the time through MySpace or IM. If they don't leave me alone, sometimes I tell my parents. *(Editor's Note: Wouldn't it be easier to set your page to private?)*

— *Donna, age 15*

I was on AIM and this random guy is like "hey" and I'm like "um do I know you?" and he said, "nope," so I looked at his profile. It had a link to porn, so I blocked him.

— *Kinsey, age 15*

Yes. On MySpace a grown man asked me to be his "friend" (it's a MySpace thing) and I replied with a no. I didn't tell my parents but I told my friends and they said that has happened to them before too. *(Editor's Note: I don't want to sound like your mom, but you are too young to have a MySpace! Even if your parents are OK with it, which I personally don't get, it is against the rules of the site to have a page if you're under the age of four- teen. See my note to Ashley, age 14, above.)*

— *Madeline, age 12*

Yes. I was online talking to my friends, and this guy started talking to me and I had no idea who he was. When I asked him who he was, he told me that I should remember because we had had cyber sex. I had never even talked to this person before.

— *Amanda, age 15*

This person started IMing me on AOL Instant Messenger, I was about 12 or 13, and I was too naive to know the difference, so I kept talking with him. After a few weeks he started freaking me out, saying he loved me and all that jazz. I blocked him real quick! Thankfully, I never gave him any of my personal info or anything. I never told my parents about it. If something like that were to happen now, my mom would be the first person I tell.

— *Amanda, age 17*

Yes, someone sent me a friend invite on MySpace and I looked at his profile to see if recognized him. I didn't know him so I deleted him. My dad was with me at the time.

— *Jennifer, age 16*

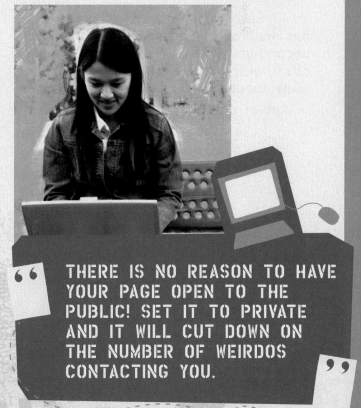

> THERE IS NO REASON TO HAVE YOUR PAGE OPEN TO THE PUBLIC! SET IT TO PRIVATE AND IT WILL CUT DOWN ON THE NUMBER OF WEIRDOS CONTACTING YOU.

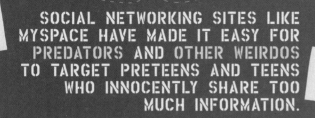
Yes, I have. I was in a Christian chat room. I guess this guy was watching me for some time. He said he was a Christian. He gained my trust. He had a Web cam and asked me if I wanted to see his face. I said "sure." I saw his face and then he brought it down to his private parts. *(Editor's Note: Girls, never go in chat rooms—even "Christian" ones. They are popular hangouts for predators. And never accept a picture or video clip from someone you have never met. Never!)*

— *Aspen, age 17*

Yes, I talked to some guy I didn't know for about ten minutes and then said I had to go. I blocked him and signed off.

— *Sara, age 14*

Yes, I have. It was really weird and he asked me inappropriate questions and I was very uncomfortable. I blocked him and logged off. I never told my parents, but I still feel guilty about it till this day.

— Jordan, age 13

Yes, he sent me a message on MySpace saying that I looked "totally hot!" and he wanted to meet me sometime because we lived in the same town. I just blocked him and completely ignored the message. I didn't tell my parents because I was afraid they would want me to get off MySpace because of it.

— *Louisa, age 14*

I was playing a game on miniclip where you had a chance to talk. I normally didn't but one time a guy wanted to know if I wanted to . . . do something that was wrong. I told my parents and now if anyone talks to me during an online game, I forfeit.

— *Lynlee, age 14*

> " MANY OF YOU ARE AFRAID YOUR PARENTS WILL FREAK OUT AND SHUT DOWN YOUR PAGE OR GROUND YOU FROM THE INTERNET, BUT YOU HAVE TO INVOLVE AN ADULT IF YOU ARE IN DANGER. "

Yes. One time I had a guy start talking to me online. He supposedly lived in my area and went to my school. At first I thought nothing of it until he started trying to get really personal. I told my dad and it ended up that this guy lived about a state away and he was in his early thirties. *(Editor's Note: Creepy! I hope girls reading this will learn from your story.)*

— *Crystal, age 16*

Well, I used to have a Xanga site open to the public. This guy started sending messages like "I would love to put you on the cam, babe," or "We should hook up," and other wrong things. I showed my mom the least embarrassing things and she said I needed to delete my site. At the time I was bummed. I thought I could just block that person. But now after looking back I know she was right.

— *Crystal, age 14*

Yes, this person would not tell me who he or she was, so I blocked them so that they couldn't send me any more messages. I made sure that I didn't tell this person any personal information, such as my name, e-mail, address, etc.

— *Perry, age 12*

Yes, there was this guy that found me through MySpace before there was the privacy option where you could block people you didn't know. I never told him anything about me because I had heard so many stories about young girls getting involved with someone from the Internet and getting raped, and sometimes killed. I chose not to tell my mom because I was too afraid of her shutting down my MySpace, and I didn't think I was in danger or at least I thought. Then I got a text message one day from him! I guess in a comment from a friend they asked me if I still had the same cell number then they listed it and that's how he got it. He was nineteen years old and this was starting to freak me out, but I never replied to his messages. Then he tried calling me and I never answered. Finally he gave up. That was last summer, but sometimes I wonder what would have happened if I replied. Now my profile is set to private and I never talk to anyone I don't know. *(Editor's Note: Good job!)*

— Amanda, age 15

Yes, there have been numerous times when boys or men will ask me where I live. Of course I don't tell them and I try to ignore them. No, I didn't tell my parents. *(Editor's Note: If you are being contacted "numerous times," why don't you set your page to private?)*

— Teresa, age 17

Yes. I was on MySpace and he commented on my pictures in my profile. I didn't tell my parents because I was ashamed that I messaged him back. *(Editor's Note: Sounds like you learned your lesson. Now, go set that page to private!)*

— Jennifer, age 16

THINK BEFORE YOU TYPE

By Vicki Courtney

a decision. She sounds hesitant on the phone and delivers the unfortunate news that they decided to make an offer to the other candidate. Your heart sinks. You really had your heart set on working at this firm. You were almost certain that you were going to get this job and had even told your parents that it was a done deal. Before hanging up, you work up your nerve and ask her why they decided on the other candidate. You tell the personnel director that

COULD THIS HAPPEN TO YOU?

Scenario 1:

You are about to graduate from law school and your dream is to be an attorney at a large prestigious law firm. You are invited to interview with one of the top three firms in the city where you desire to practice. The interview goes great and they basically tell you that they have narrowed it down to two candidates and you are one of them. Before you leave, they give strong indication that you are the frontrunner. They tell you that they will call you in a few days if they are going to extend an offer. A few days go by and the call doesn't come. Finally, you can't stand the suspense of not knowing so you pick up the phone and you call the personnel director. You politely ask her if they have come to

her information could possibly help you in future interviews. And then, she drops the bomb. "Well, if you really want to know . . . we had decided on you. However, we wanted to make certain that you would be a good match with the values and integrity that we deem to be important in this firm, so we decided to take a look at your Facebook page. This is a standard procedure in our firm and we can easily access a student's page through alumni at the firm or one of our college interns. What we found on your page raised some red flags and even though you interviewed well, we just couldn't take a chance. I'm very sorry. I only share this with you as it is very common for employers to look up potential candidates on MySpace and Facebook, and it may continue to be a factor in your not getting a job." You are speechless, but you regain your composure, politely thank her, and hang up the phone. You pull up your Facebook page, and for the first time, you view it through different eyes—the eyes of a potential employer. On your wall one of your friends has jokingly posted, "Hey Amanda, you slut! I haven't seen you in forever—let's hang out soon!" There are plenty of other expletives and sexually suggestive comments on the page. And then there are the pictures . . . several of you drinking at a party, another one of you kissing your boyfriend, and another of you and a friend leaning over in your bikini tops exposing your

cleavage for all to see. It seemed funny at the time. But you're not laughing now. Through tears, you begin to remove the evidence . . . one picture and one comment at a time.

Scenario 2:

You meet a really nice guy who finds you on MySpace. He goes to a different high school in your city and says he's a sophomore just like you. Before long, you are talking about meeting somewhere. You're not stupid, so you set up the meeting at the mall and make sure that your friends will be there with you. The meeting time arrives, and he never shows. When you get home later, he messages you and says that he chickened out because he didn't tell you the complete truth when you met online. He tells you that he's really older than

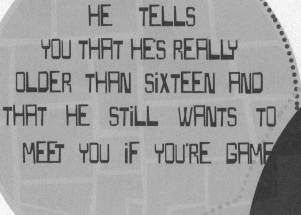

HE TELLS YOU THAT HE'S REALLY OLDER THAN SIXTEEN AND THAT HE STILL WANTS TO MEET YOU IF YOU'RE GAME

sixteen and that he still wants to meet you if you're game. When you ask him how old he is, he tells you that he's twenty-five and that he listed the high school he used to attend and a fake age because he wants to meet younger girls. Now, you're totally creeped out and you tell him no way will you ever meet him. He pleads with you to meet him and says that if you get to know him, he knows it will still work out. You tell him no way and sign off. The next day you head to work at the dry cleaners down the block from your school. You're excited because you are working the same shift as your best friend. The first hour is pretty busy but then it slows down and you and Sarah have a chance to catch up. You tell her all about the creep you met on MySpace and how you refused to meet him. She tells you to block him just to be safe and you agree to do it when you get home. At that moment, your cell phone buzzes with a text. You look and it's a message from him. The message says, "when is ur break?" Sarah is busy at the counter with a customer who just walked in. Then you notice a guy sitting outside in a jeep and you remember that he said he drove a jeep. He smiles at you. How did he know you were at work? You had told him where you worked, which you now realize, was a huge mistake. You had also posted your cell phone number. And then you remembered that Sarah had posted a message to you last night saying she was psyched that you guys had the same shift the next day. What else did this guy know? You text him back and tell him to get lost—you don't ever want to meet him. You warn him that if he contacts you again, you're calling the police. He reads the text and screeches out of the parking lot. By then, the customer is gone and Sarah can tell you're upset. You tell her what happened and she suggests that you tell your parents. You are super scared this guy is going to stalk you but you can't imagine telling your parents. They will ground you for life for talking to him in the first

YOU ARE SUPER SCARED THIS GUY IS GOING TO STALK YOU BUT YOU CAN'T IMAGINE TELLING YOUR PARENTS. THEY WILL GROUND YOU FOR LIFE FOR TALKING TO HIM IN THE FIRST PLACE AND PROBABLY MAKE YOU SHUT DOWN YOUR MYSPACE PAGE.

place and probably make you shut down your MySpace page. After work, on the way home, you keep checking your rearview mirror for his jeep. At one point, a jeep pulls up beside you at a stoplight and you are shaking uncontrollably. You have your cell phone ready. It's not him. Finally, you pull into your driveway. You can't live like this. You decide to tell your parents . . .

Scenario 3:

Fast-forward ten years from now. You have met the man of your dreams and he asks you to meet his parents. You can picture yourself with this guy for the rest of your life. He is a godly man who somehow managed to stay committed to Christ through his high school and college years. You, however, have a different story. Even though you were raised going to church, you ended up in the wrong crowd in high school and partied it up. Once you got to college, you realized how empty those years were and came back to the path of God. It wasn't easy. You found a church,

HE SAID HIS MOTHER HAD UTILIZED A SOFTWARE PROGRAM TO PULL UP OLD CACHED AWAY COPIES OF PAGES ON THE INTERNET FROM YEARS PRIOR.

girl in the college group that didn't want a date with him. But he chose you. After a few months of dating, you told him about your past. He was understanding and reassured you that it was behind you now. He reminded you of 2 Corinthians 5:17 which says, "Therefore if anyone is in Christ, there is a new creation; old things have passed away, and look, new things have come." This is the kind of guy girls dream of marrying. And now it was a possibility, but first, it was time to meet the parents.

The day before you leave, he comes over and seems upset. He was hesitant to tell you, but finally you are able to drag it out of him. He said his mother had utilized a software program to pull up old cached away copies of pages on the Internet from years prior. You had heard of software like this but didn't know the extent of what it could actually do. His mom had easily pulled up your MySpace page from your high school years—even though it had been shut down long ago. She was deeply

joined a small group Bible study, and gave up parties and drinking. Years later, your new Christian friends could hardly believe the stories you told them about your past. Your regretted the mistakes you had made but knew God had forgiven you. And then you met him. He was considered the biggest catch at your church. There was hardly a

disturbed by what she saw and in need of reassurance from her son that you had really changed. He assured her that you had and that she would see for herself what a wonderful girl you were when you met in person. You could hardly breathe when he finished telling you. Never in a million years when you had your MySpace page did you imagine that it could come back to haunt you years later, even after you had shut it down. You cringed as you

remembered back on your page and how sickened you yourself were when you looked over it after committing your life to Christ a few years later. It had felt so good to get rid of it, like you were making a fresh start. But it didn't really go away . . .

DON'T THINK IT CAN HAPPEN?

THINK AGAIN.

Stories similar to the first two scenarios are making the news almost every day. In fact, just recently, the organization I founded was hiring for a new position. Out of about twenty résumés we received, we ended up eliminating four possible candidates based on background checks we did on MySpace and Facebook. And the third scenario is highly likely, given that nothing you ever post on the Web really goes away. The capability already exists to view pages on the Web that have been changed or removed. Police detectives use it regularly when investigating crimes, and it's not unreasonable to think that the same technology will be available to the general public in the years to come.

I am not saying that social networking sites are evil. Rather, I am pleading with you to be responsible if you choose to use them. Are you sharing too much information? Have you shared details that enable a predator or stalker to find you and, if they choose, follow you and possibly harm you? Is your page

something that you would be comfortable showing to a potential employer, your pastor, neighbor, grandmother, or boyfriend's parents? Are you posting things that may come back to haunt you years later, even after you have shut down your page or removed comments and pictures? Of course, the most important question is, "Would my page be pleasing to God?" In fact, here is a good rule of thumb—would others who look at your page know that you are a Christian based on what they find? Even if you state that you are a Christian somewhere on the page, would your comments, friends' comments, links, or pictures line up with your faith. Or would they scream, "Hypocrite!" ★

> "Let your light shine before men, that they may see your good deeds and praise your Father in heaven."
> Matthew 5:16 (NIV)

Survey
Pet Peeves
by Vicki Courtney

Grrrr . . . It's Time to Sound Off!

The dictionary defines pet peeve as "a particular or recurring source of irritation." For me, it's people with bad cell phone manners (thus, the quiz on page 138). Look, I love my cell phone just as much as the next guy and I can't imagine life without it. But sometimes I want to imagine others without theirs.

Especially the guy last week who was on my plane and carried on a loud conversation with someone about his kidney stone. Please, I didn't want to know that—can't it wait until he's in a more private location? I'm sure I speak for the person on the receiving end when I say, "Spare us." Or maybe I started to crack when I entered the ladies restroom to find yet again someone chatting on her phone. I don't care how important the matter is—please don't call me if there are toilets flushing in the background and a woman in the next stall asking two-year-old little Johnny if he made a "poo in the potty." Bad idea. Or maybe it is carrying on a conversation with someone only to have the person take the call or check a text message when his or her phone vibrates. If it's an emergency, that's understandable, but most are unnecessary distractions that can wait until the conversation has ended. The next time it happens, I just may walk away and dial their cell phone number, since that seems to be the best way to get their undivided attention.

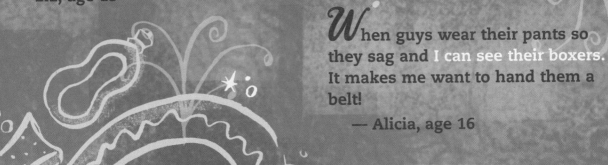

Ewww~

So, what about you? Do you have a pet peeve? We asked that question in our survey and now, it's your turn to sound off!

When I'm doing the dishes and people walk by and put their dirty plates in the dishwater rather than putting it beside the sink so I can rinse it off and not have chucks of food floating around in the dishwater.

— Liz, age 15

When guys wear their pants so they sag and I can see their boxers. It makes me want to hand them a belt!

— Alicia, age 16

When parents are trying to tell their children in public places to stop what they are doing and behave. The parents just keep telling them to stop and raise their voices louder and louder in the process. Meanwhile, they are creating a scene. They will not even try to be reasonable with them in explaining to them what it is they are doing wrong.

— Melissa, age 14

My little brother Michael eats with his mouth open! He is really cute and all and he really likes to sit by me. But, then I end up with casserole all over my shirt from him talking and spraying it all over me.
SO ANNOYING & GROSS

— Natalie, age 12

When people talk during a movie!

— Hailey, age 13

Blah Blah Blah!

icky sticky

My biggest pet peeve is skinny girls talking about how "fat" they are. It just shows a lack of confidence on their part.

— Laura, age 17

A mark left on a whiteboard when people are erasing it.

— Haley, age 12

When people drive about 10 mph below the speed limit.

— Rebecca, age 17

Habitual nose pickers; or people who talk REALLY LOUD even though you are standing right there next to them.

— Becca, age 16

When people stick gum under the desks at school.

— Ashley, age 12

I can't stand when people get right beside me and/or look over my shoulder and/or listen in while I'm doing something. (Ex: talk on the phone, draw, surf on the Internet, IM, e-mail, read, and all kinds of things.)

— Meagan, age 14

People who make a smacking sound (apparently without their knowledge) after each sentence before they begin the next one.
— Laurel, age 17

Annoying!

When people chew gum and you can hear them chewing it and then they make these really loud bubbles. It's horrible!
— Elizabeth, age 16

When you're talking to someone and their cell phone rings and they act like you're not even there.
— Maggie, age 12 *

weigh in @ virtuous reality .com

These are a few of my un-favorite things.

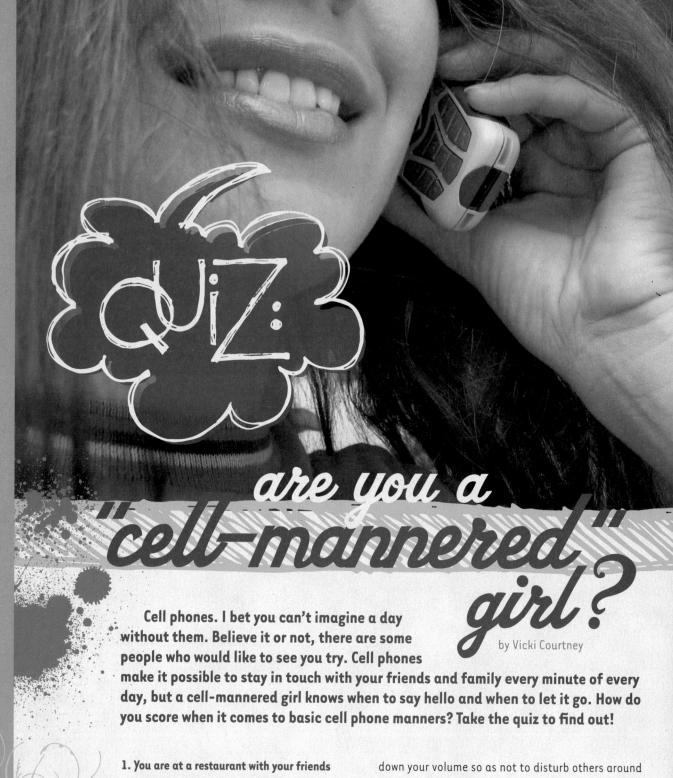

QUIZ:

are you a "cell-mannered" girl?

by Vicki Courtney

Cell phones. I bet you can't imagine a day without them. Believe it or not, there are some people who would like to see you try. Cell phones make it possible to stay in touch with your friends and family every minute of every day, but a cell-mannered girl knows when to say hello and when to let it go. How do you score when it comes to basic cell phone manners? Take the quiz to find out!

1. You are at a restaurant with your friends (yes, fast food still counts!) and your cell phone goes off. It's your best friend and she's been at camp for two weeks. You . . .

   a) answer the phone at the table screaming with excitement and tell her to come meet you at the restaurant.

   b) tell your friends, "Guys, it's Emily and she's been at camp for two weeks. I have to get this" and you take the call but turn down your volume so as not to disturb others around you.

   c) ditto to the above except you excuse yourself from the table to take the call in a quieter place, so others can enjoy their meal.

2. You are in church and you forgot to turn off your phone. It vibrates in your bag indicating you have a text message. You . . .

   a) check it out and send a quick reply. Besides, it'll make the long sermon go by faster.

b) check to see who it is. You can call them back when the service is over and you're headed to youth group.

c) fumble in your bag, grab it, and turn it off quickly. Next time you will leave it in the car so it never happens again. Nothing should distract you or others from giving God the time he deserves.

3. You are in a movie theater and the previews are on. Your phone vibrates and you . . .

a) answer it and chat for about a minute telling your friend where you are and who you're with. No one likes the previews anyway, right?

b) send a quick text to your friend telling her where you are. You can trade a few text messages before the movie starts.

c) turn your phone off. You didn't pay seven bucks to sit in a movie theater and talk or text.

4. Your plane just landed and is heading for the designated gate. You want to make sure your mom is outside waiting to meet you. You . . .

a) turn on your phone, dial her number, and begin to tell her about your trip while those around you are trapped in the cabin and forced to listen.

b) turn on your phone, dial her number, and very quietly ask her if she is there under your breath. When she asks you how the trip went and you tell her that you're still on the plane and you will tell her all about it when you get in the car.

c) wait until you get off the plane and dial her number when you're on your way to the baggage claim area.

5. You are talking with one of your friends and she is sharing about her painful break-up with her boyfriend. Your phone rings. You . . .

a) tell your friend, "Hang on a sec. I have to get this."

b) check to see who it is while she's talking. You don't plan to answer it, but you need to know who to call back when you're free.

c) ignore it. Nothing is more important than giving your friend your full undivided attention.

6. You are at a party and you were supposed to meet one of your friends but she's not there yet. You . . .

a) dial her number while waiting in line to get some food. When she answers, you scream, "Where are you and what is taking you so long?" You keep talking while filling up your plate and shoving nachos into your mouth.

b) dial her number and ask her when she'll be there. Everyone else in the room is busy talking and you're feeling left out.

b) keep the conversation going until you see that it's almost your turn to order. You tell her you will call her back after you order your drink.

c) tell her you have to go before you step into the store. You don't want to interrupt others with your conversation and besides, it's too hard to talk, pay, and drink at the same time.

c) make a point to meet new people. If your friend is still not there in another 15 minutes, you will step outside and give her a quick call to make sure everything is all right.

7. You are chatting away with a friend on the phone and pull into your favorite coffee shop for a vanilla latte. The drive-thru line is a mile long so you decide to go inside to order. You . . .

a) keep the conversation going while walking in, standing in line, and tell her to hold on a sec when it's your turn to order. Now, that's multi-tasking!

8. You ride with your mom to pick your aunt up at the airport. Once in the car, she and your mom begin chatting away in the front seat. Your phone rings. You . . .

a) answer the phone and begin your own little chat-fest.

b) answer the phone, talk for a few minutes, and then tell your friend you need to go visit with your aunt.

c) ignore the call and join in on the conversation with your mom and aunt. You can talk to your friends anytime, but your aunt only comes to town once a year. Besides, it's rude to subject others to your conversation when they are trapped in a small space with you and unable to escape.

9. You're watching a movie with some friends and your phone goes off. It's your mom so you better answer. You . . .

a) answer it during the movie and talk to her while your friends are shushing you.

(b) you answer it and tell your mom you'll call her back after the movie.

c) you step out of the room and answer the phone in a more private location. That way you can focus on what your mom is saying without interrupting your friends.

10. Your mom is asking about your day and your phone vibrates with a text message from a friend. She is supposed to text you the times of movie you're planning to see that night. You . . .

a) check your phone for the text and send your friend a quick text back. Mom won't mind, right?

(b) politely interrupt your mom and tell her you're expecting a text about the movie times. You ask her if it's OK if you check the message and reply.

c) ignore the message. It will still be there when you're done talking to your mom.

11. You are at the mall and talking on your phone with one of your friends. You have to go to the restroom. You . . .

a) keep on talking while taking care of business. So, a few potties flush in the background—who hasn't heard that before?

b) keep talking up until it's time to walk into the stall, announcing in the restroom, "I'll call you right back. I gotta go to the bathroom!"

(c) don't even think about walking through the bathroom door while still talking on the phone. I mean, it's just wrong on so many levels.

12. You are at a concert and your favorite band is on stage. You . . .

a) scream "Oh my gosh—this is Jennifer's favorite song!" You dial her number and start screaming into the phone telling her where you are. You hold up the phone for her to hear the song.

b) start taking multiple pictures of the band with your camera phone.

(c) enjoy the song and respect the rights of others around you to also enjoy the song. I mean, you all paid big bucks to hear the band live so it only makes sense to fully enjoy the experience.

~~IIII~~   ~~HHH~~ II

COUNT THE NUMBER OF As, Bs, AND Cs YOU HAVE.

IF YOU HAVE MOSTLY C: Congratulations, when it comes to cell phone manners, you take the prize. Not many girls your age would fall into this category. Keep up the good work and maybe others will learn from your example!

IF YOU HAVE MOSTLY B AND C: You're cell phone manners could use some improvement. If you're on the phone or someone calls or texts you and you're not quite sure if it's an appropriate setting to talk, err on the side of etiquette and practice some restraint.

IF YOU HAVE MOSTLY B AND A: Yikes. You err on the side of rude when it comes to cell phone manners. Chances are, you're not being rude intentionally and you've never really questioned how your behavior impacts others around you. Make a concentrated effort to think of others and kick this bad habit.

IF YOU HAVE MOSTLY A: When you look up *rude* in the dictionary, your picture is beside it. Your lack of manners and consideration of others shows that you only care about one thing—YOU! Pray and ask God to help you put others before yourself. More important, back it up with action. You can do it! ✱

Survey: Life with No Regrets?

by Vicki Courtney

Call me weird, but I like to read the obituaries in the newspaper. My family makes fun of me, but I find it fascinating to read about people who have passed on. It's pretty humbling when you stop and think that our lives will some day be summed up in a few brief paragraphs in a newspaper. Like one guy I read about whose family member said, "He wanted to live life with no regrets and he did just that." Hmm . . . that one sentence really got me thinking. **Is it really possible to live life without a single regret?** I don't think so. Surely, this guy at some point in his life said an unkind word to someone. I'm pretty sure he lied, cheated, or lusted in his heart. No one is perfect so we know he committed sins. Did he not regret them? Did he not regret when his actions hurt others? Maybe I'm overanalyzing this, but I don't think I can admire someone who "lives life with no regrets."

Some of the biggest regrets of my life came during my high school and college years. "If I could go back and do it over again . . ." Have you ever heard someone say that? Probably so. In life, we will make mistakes. Some people will make more than others, but we will all make them. It seems to me that the key is to live life with as few regrets as possible. That means learning from the mistakes we make and moving on. **Philippians 3:13–14** says, **"Brothers, I do not consider myself to have taken hold of it. But one thing I do: forgetting what is behind and reaching forward to what is ahead, I pursue as my goal the prize promised by God's heavenly call in Christ Jesus."** Sounds to me like a good remedy for regrets: forgetting what is behind and reaching forward to what is ahead.

What about you? What's your biggest regret?

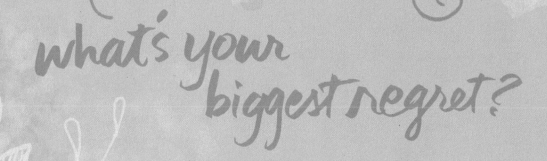
what's your biggest regret?

Having sex before marriage!
— *Heather, age 17*

Telling a girl a secret and finding out she
wasn't a real friend. — *Liz, age 15*

My mom and I were in a coffee shop and
they were handing out free ice cream.
There was only one left and I took it. Just
then I realized that a homeless man was about
to take it. I kept it anyways and later I felt so
bad. — *Natalie, age 12*

My biggest regret would have to be . . .
talking behind my friend's back
more than once. — *Melissa, age 14*

I don't have a biggest regret, but I always regret
lying to or yelling at my parents.
— *Kelsi, age 14*

My biggest regret is not talking to
two girls on my cheer team
our freshman year.
— *Kristin, age 16*

That I have anorexia.
— *Kristen, age 15*

Getting drunk at a party.
— *Kirsten, age 13*

I have two:
1) Not waiting until marriage.
2) Not getting rid of my ex-boyfriend
sooner! — *Amanda, age 18*

When I go to church camp, I learn so much,
then I come home and I don't change
anything. Basically I just have a camp high.
— *Hannah, age 16*

Not spending enough "quality time" with
people and not having enough heart-to-heart
talks with my sis. She's leaving for college
this summer and I'm just starting to
realize all the stuff we never did.
— **Mary, age 15**

My biggest regret is that I haven't spent
enough time with my grandparents who
are starting to show their age.
— *Becky, age 15*

Going back to a guy that wasn't good for me.
— Emily, age 14

I always judge people. I want to stop,
but sometimes words just slip out.
— **Hannah, age 12**

Being mad at my dad and then he
died unexpectedly. I didn't get to
tell him that I loved him. — Amber, age 14

My biggest regret is probably giving a big piece of my heart emotionally to a guy who amazed me because he was such a godly guy, but who was still pretty immature. Which I should have expected since he's only in high school! God knew what he was doing when he designed relationships for later in life!
— Julie, age 14

One of my biggest regrets is not trying hard enough in school. I don't make bad grades. I just know that I could do better.
— Amberly, age 16

My biggest regret is that I told this guy I dated I loved him, when I really didn't. I said it because I didn't want him to feel bad. — Laurel, age 17

Losing my parents' trust by lying.
— Becca, age 16

Hanging out and being involved with people that drink and do bad things.
— Amber, age 19

My regret is a regret but also a blessing from God. Last year I thought about killing myself. I decided I would starve myself and I began to do so. A friend convinced me to stop and since then I've been able to look back at that time and say to myself, If God can get me through that, he can get me through anything.
— Kaitlyn, age 13 ★

Survey: TALK ABOUT embarrassing!!

BY VICKI COURTNEY

We've all had it happen.

No one can escape embarrassing moments. True, some are more embarrassing than others, but everyone has a story about a heart-beating-palm-sweating-cheeks-blushing moment where time stood still and you wanted to curl up and die.

I had an embarrassing moment happen recently when I was being interviewed on a live radio show. For 15 minutes I talked to the host, Don, about my new book. Now, this wasn't one of those little radio shows in Smalltown, USA with a listening audience as big as your English class.

No, it was a big kahuna show where people tuned in everyday because they liked Don the host because he was interesting and put on a good show. Only problem was that the host's name wasn't "Don." It was "Dan." At the end of the interview, the sound technician very kindly informed me of that small detail when we were off the air. I had called the host the wrong name throughout the entire interview. Ugh. Talk about embarrassing . . .

We may not be able to control those unexpected embarrassing moments, but we can choose how we react to them. In the situation above, I had two choices: 1) I could dwell on it for the rest of the day and beat myself up, or 2) I could laugh my head off and move on. I chose #2 and now, when I think about it, I crack up. I'm not sure Don (whoops, I mean Dan) is cracking up yet, but oh well. Life is too short to dwell on such silly matters. And that is exactly what I told myself in the moments that immediately followed my embarrassing moment. The truth is, while it may be extremely embarrassing at the time, no one is really dwelling on it as much as you. Within moments, it is usually quickly forgotten. So, Dan, if you are reading this, I am really, really sorry I called you Don on your show, and I would love it if you would give me another chance in the future. If it makes you feel better, you can call me "Courtney" the entire show. It happens all the time. ☺

WHILE IT MAY BE *extremely* EMBARRASSING AT THE TIME, NO ONE IS REALLY DWELLING ON IT AS *much as you.*

★ ★ ★

I was in church and had just gotten back from a senior trip to Washington, D.C. I was wearing an "I ♥ D.C." shirt. Our pastor's name just so happens to have the initials "DC." He announced that he was preaching the next evening at a conference and told everyone that was planning to come to wear a T-shirt like mine. Then he called me to the front of the sanctuary to show the whole church my shirt.
I turned ten shades of red.

Amanda.
age 18

What about you? Do you have an embarrassing moment to share?

In the fifth grade, we had "the talk" (if you know what I mean). That day at lunch, we had hamburgers and I ended up spilling ketchup all over the front of my khaki pants! I had to walk around for the rest of the day with a coat zipped up around my waist!

Jennifer. age 13

My most embarrassing moment would have to be when I thought that Sonic did home deliveries because I saw a sign on their door that said, "No deliveries between 11:30–1:30." I didn't know the sign was for the people delivering the food to them!

Amber. age 19

I was student directing a play in eighth grade and it was closing night. There were a pair of twins involved in the production and one had a speaking part and the other was involved in the crew. They came up to me and told me they were going to switch places. I went to talk to the supervising teacher and she confronted the girls with me and we told them that they would not be able to switch parts. The girls got upset and the one with the speaking part refused to go on stage. The teacher shoved a script in my hand and pushed me on stage. I had to play the main part dressed in all black (crew attire) and reading from a script! It was really embarrassing because I hate being up in front of people.

Sarah, age 17

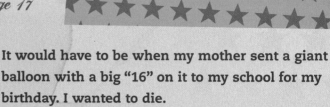

It would have to be when my mother sent a giant balloon with a big "16" on it to my school for my birthday. I wanted to die.

Rachel, age 16

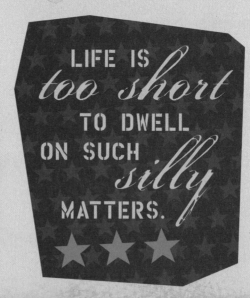

LIFE IS *too short* TO DWELL ON SUCH *silly* MATTERS.

★ ★ ★

One time my friend was joking around with her mom and threw her bra at her. Her mom picked it up and threw it back at her, but it ended up hitting me and the hooks got caught in my hair!

Amy, age 14

The most embarrassing moment I can think of would have to be when my friend got a new digital camera and we took a ton of crazy pictures with it. I was in my pj's and my hair and makeup looked terrible. We took about twenty pictures of us making weird faces. Apparently, my friend's older brother had a friend over and used the camera. The brother's friend asked for the pictures they had taken and my friend's brother gave him the whole memory card! I had a little bit of a crush on the older brother's friend and I about had a heart attack when I got an e-mail from him saying, "Hey, Matt e-mailed me some pictures, and half of them are of you looking goofy!"

Julie, age 14

I was the new girl after we moved last year and no one could ever remember my name at school. They just called me "new girl."

Maggie, age 12

I am captain of our school's flag corps for marching band, and we practice during first period. We had just started a rifle line and I was tossing my rifle up in a horizontal toss and the rifle came back and hit me in the nose. Everyone rushed over to see what had happened and asked if I was OK. I said I was fine but then someone pointed out that my face had started to swell! It stayed that way the rest of the school day.

Christine, age 18

My most embarrassing moment was when I was in seventh grade. I was at junior high church camp and I had a huge crush on this guy. Some of my friends decided to write him a love note from me and gave it to him without me knowing. He came up to me and was like "I only like you as a friend." I had no idea what he was talking about. It was embarrassing at the time, but now when we all look back on it, we laugh.

Amberly, age 16 ★